DISRUPTIVE WOMEN

Edited by **VIVIENNE PORRITT,**
LISA HANNAY & NATASHA HILTON

DISRUPTIVE
WOMEN

A WomenEd
Guide to
Equitable
Action in
Education

CORWIN

CORWIN

A SAGE Publishing Company

1 Oliver's Yard
55 City Road
London EC1Y 1SP

CORWIN
A Sage company
2455 Teller Road
Thousand Oaks, California 91320
(800)233-9936
www.corwin.com

Unit No 323-333, Third Floor, F-Block
International Trade Tower, Nehru Place
New Delhi 110 019

8 Marina View Suite 43-053
Asia Square Tower 1
Singapore 018960

Editor: James Clark
Assistant editor: Esosa Otabor
Production editor: Martin Fox
Copyeditor: Christine Bitten
Proofreader: Leigh Smithson
Indexer: Judith Lavender
Marketing manager: Dilhara Attygalle
Cover design: Wendy Scott
Typeset by: C&M Digitals (P) Ltd, Chennai, India
Printed and bound by
CPI Group (UK) Ltd, Croydon, CR0 4YY

British Library Cataloguing in Publication data

A catalogue record for this book is available from the British Library

ISBN 978-1-5296-7327-2
ISBN 978-1-5296-7326-5 (pbk)

CONTENTS

ABOUT THE EDITORS

Vivienne Porritt OBE FRSA FCCT Joyously, Vivienne Porritt is a co-founder, trustee and Global Strategic Leader of WomenEd, a global charity which empowers and elevates aspiring and existing women leaders in education.

As a leadership consultant, Vivienne supports school and trust leaders with vision, strategy, professional learning and development, impact evaluation and Diversity, Equity, Inclusion and Justice (DEIJ), and she is also a coach and holds several governance roles.

Vivienne is a former secondary Headteacher and Vice President of the Chartered College of Teaching as well as Director for School Partnerships at University College London, Institute of Education. She writes for practitioner and academic journals and is co-editor of *10% Braver: Inspiring Women to Lead Education* (Sage, 2019) and *Being 10% Braver* (Sage/Corwin, 2021).

Lisa Hannay Lisa is an Assistant Principal in Calgary, Alberta, Canada. Lisa's WomenEd journey began at a conference many years ago when she attended two WomenEd sessions. There was a palpable energy that was uplifting and empowering. Lisa discovered that the mission and values of WomenEd aligned beautifully with her own desire to create disruption and to challenge the status quo. Lisa wrote a chapter for the second WomenEd book, *Being 10% Braver*, and has contributed to articles spotlighting women in leadership along with Vivienne Porritt. Lisa is one of the trustees and Global Strategic Leaders for WomenEd and gets up every morning to cause a little good trouble.

Natasha Hilton My journey in education began back in 2006, when I eagerly stepped into the bustling halls of inner-city London schools. I immersed myself in the dynamic landscape of education, refining my skills and nurturing a deep passion for learning. In 2014, fuelled by a desire for new experiences and challenges, I made the bold decision to embark on an international adventure. With my family by my side, we embarked on a journey that led us to Oman, where I continued my career in education within a global context and by 2020 during the height of the pandemic my journey took me to Qatar where I am now based.

As I navigated the intricacies of international education, I found myself drawn to a new mission: supporting and empowering women in leadership roles. Over the years, my first-hand experiences have highlighted the barriers that women often face on their leadership journey. Driven by a dedication to equality and progress, I have committed myself to breaking down these barriers and championing the advancement of women in the field.

Through mentorship, advocacy, and a relentless pursuit of change, I strive to create a more inclusive and equitable environment for all aspiring female leaders in education as a trustee and Global Strategic Leader for WomenEd.

ABOUT THE CONTRIBUTORS

Angeline Aow is an international educator, DEIJ consultant, pedagogical leader, and author of *Becoming a Totally Inclusive School: A Guide for Teachers and School Leaders*, as well as a WomenEd Network Leader for Germany.

Ruth Astley is a passionate advocate for family-friendly schools, promoting flexible working and championing women in education as Assistant Headteacher (Teaching and Learning) at a secondary school in South East England. She is also Assistant Maths Hub Lead for Sussex and a WomenEd network leader. She has three children and has worked part-time for 10 years in middle and senior leader roles.

Radha Badhan has been in teaching for 11 years in both the private and state sectors and is proud to be one of the youngest global majority Headteachers in the UK, being Headteacher of Bringhurst Primary School.

Yasmine Baker, diagnosed with ADHD two years ago, brings a unique perspective to her role as an English educator at a secondary school outside Birmingham, England and to driving positive change within the school community, fostering an inclusive and supportive learning environment for all.

Amy Bowdler is a Deputy Headteacher in Gateshead, North East England and is a passionate advocate for women in leadership.

Suzanne Brown is a senior lecturer in teacher education. Her research interests lie in teacher recruitment and retention, including support for flexible working, teaching, and the menopause, and making schools places where people want to work.

Joyce I-Hui Chen is a Quality Enhancement Manager and a Teacher Centre Manager as well as a researcher in the higher education sector.

Wendy Cobb is an international teacher, educator and author. She has also worked in primary and secondary schools across Kent, London and Essex in a variety of teaching, leadership, advisory and coaching roles.

Hannah Duncan is a Senior Lecturer in Primary Education at Canterbury Christ Church University, UK, having previously taught in primary schools in Kent and

London. She is currently researching male and female teachers' experiences of flexible working in England for her PhD.

Stephani Dupree's journey as a woman who entered a male-dominated industry has taken her from a junior to a Fellow, and she is driven to achieve equality and equity. To raise the profile of gender gaps and working disparity of women has been her source of passion.

Maggie Eldridge-Mrotzek is a lifelong educator: teacher, school leader, inspector, consultant and senior adviser.

Loretta Fernando-Smith is a mother, educator and Third Culture Kid and WomenEd Network Leader based in Germany. Her experiences of straddling several cultures as a child, adult, parent and educator have made her curious about how people negotiate belonging in different spaces.

Maz Foucher is a former Assistant Headteacher with over 20 years' experience in teaching and leadership. She is now Devon Regional Representative for the Maternity Teacher Paternity Teacher (MTPT) Project.

Liz Free is CEO and Director at the International School Rheintal in Switzerland, WomenEd Trustee and Global Strategic Leader, *Tes* finalist for International Headteacher of the Year 2024 and advocate for the global teaching profession.

Jess Gosling began the WomenEd network in Taiwan and is an experienced teacher and middle leader of a growing early years department in an international school.

Bianca Greenhalgh is an executive Headteacher in the UK. She is passionate about creating spaces for women in leadership.

Rebecca Hoyes has 20 years' experience in teaching, inspired by a family of teachers. She is currently Director of Teaching and Learning at an independent school in Surrey, England, and mother to two young children. She is passionate about geography, supporting early career teachers, leading training and professional development, and inspiring female colleagues in the workplace.

Jenetta Hurst is a Professional Development Lead and Senior Leader in a secondary school and has also developed a music consultancy.

Miriam Hussain is a Senior Leader and teacher of English in the West Midlands, England and is passionate about closing the attainment gap and staff development and is a Teach First Ambassador.

Kerry Jordan-Daus is the CEO of Veritas Multi Academy Trust. Prior to this she was a senior leader in higher education. Her research interests are in gender and leadership and she is a Network Leader for WomenEd.

Katrina Kerry is a Headteacher who continues to strive for equality, ambition and success for staff and pupils with professional urgency.

Jess Mahdavi-Gladwell (CPsychol AFBPsS CTeach MCCT FHEA) is Deputy Head of a Primary Pupil Referral Unit (PRU) and lives in Kent, England. She is driven to seek the best outcomes and opportunities for children who have experienced exclusion in mainstream school settings.

Abigail Mann is a Deputy Headteacher with a keen interest in coaching and wellbeing, both of which underpin her leadership of teaching and learning, curriculum, and staff development.

Katy Marsh-Davies, PhD, is a Senior Lecturer with Hull University Business School and co-editor of the book *Teachers and Teaching Post-COVID*, published by Routledge (2023).

Esther Mustamu-Daniels, a proud Moluccan, has worked in education and with young people for over 20 years and is committed to supporting fellow educators in developing their understanding of race and power to deliver a more equitable and just society for future generations.

Lindsay Patience is a part-time teacher of economics and business, and co-founder of Flexible Teacher Talent, an organisation which promotes flexible working in the education sector. Lindsay is the co-author (with Lucy Rose) of *Flex Education: A guide for flexible working in schools* (Sage/Corwin, 2022).

Parm Plummer has been in education for nearly 30 years working in schools in the UK and abroad, and is now an Assistant Headteacher in Jersey and a passionate advocate for WomenEd as a Global Strategic Leader and network leader for WomenEd Jersey.

Sue Prickett is a WomenEd Network Leader and a leader of finance and operations across five special needs schools and a champion for the many roles of school business leadership with a commitment to highlighting the need for funding reforms in special educational needs in the UK.

Aimee Quickfall is the Head of School of the School of Education at Leeds Trinity University and is also Cormac's mum.

Nasima Riazat is Curriculum Lead for Business Studies, School Careers Lead, Personal, Health, Social and Economic Education (PHSE) and Relationships and Sex Education (RSE), and Head of Business and Technology Education Council (BTEC)/Vocational Studies at Pendle Vale College, North West England, and is passionate about achieving lasting change through advocacy.

Derry Richardson is an educator, author and leader in a local authority, raising the profile of professional learning to improve life chances of children, young people and learners.

Kiran Satti is a Senior Leader in West Midlands, England and a Network Leader for WomenEd. She relentlessly believes in the power of education to enable, empower and inspire positive impact on the life chances of young people.

Angela Schofield is Programme Development Lead for Excelsior MAT in England, leading on oracy, disadvantage strategy, teaching and learning, and research engagement.

Azuraye Williams is a senior leader within a primary school and leads on Diversity, Equity, Inclusion and Belonging across her trust of 23 schools. She speaks about her passion for representation and inclusion within schools for both the staff and the children. She recently won an award for her services to education around diversity.

Haley Yearwood has, since becoming a teacher of English and Drama in 2008 and being diagnosed with multiple sclerosis that same year, tackled the complexities of working in demanding secondary schools in West London. Haley leads safeguarding and mental wellbeing, while navigating her leadership journey as a woman of colour.

Helen Young has taught in secondary schools in the UK for 27 years and had a global influence through her roles with Cambridge University Press and the BBC. Additionally, she is a Subject Matter Specialist for Ofqual and an Educational Consultant working with schools and businesses.

ACKNOWLEDGEMENTS

In May 2024, WomenEd became 9 years old. What an amazing journey we are on, with this our third book, and a global community of over 50,000. We are so proud that there are greater numbers of women being 10% braver and smashing the gender stereotypes that lead to systematic inequity for women educators and leaders. Yet there is so much more to do, with women around the world haunted by abuse and violence.

In tackling the inequity we face, we want to acknowledge our sisters in disruption – Keziah, Liz, and Parm for all their support and brilliant work as Global Strategic Leaders. Thank you also to our wonderful family of network leaders and the magnificent WomenEd community around the world for your support and engagement. We send our special thanks to our website wizard, Gemma. Thanks, as ever, to James Clark and Sage for their constant belief and support, and to Wendy Scott for a brilliant cover!

To you, the reader, we offer our sincerest gratitude for choosing to engage with this book. The forces of conformity would rather you didn't. They fear the empowerment and elevation of women, the amplification of their voices.

Those who want to maintain the status quo in education don't want women to find their voices, and they certainly don't want them using them. In this book, our authors have wielded their voices by telling their stories and we have weaved them into a powerful message of change.

Now we invite you to join us. Embrace your voice, become a disruptor in your own right for yourself and your organization. Together we can shatter the constraints of the status quo and forge a path towards true equity and empowerment.

Your voice matters.

Use your superpowers boldly.

Vivienne's Acknowledgements

I feel very privileged to have played a part in all three of our books and this book especially shows me the success of our mantra of 10% braver. The authors show real courage in being prepared to share their experiences and concerns, and how to disrupt the status quo so more women can grow and become leaders without the fear of facing sexism and bias. Thank you for this bravery which is having a significant impact for women and for education.

Thank you to Tony and Julie who, as ever, propped me up as our deadline approached, and it's been an absolute joy to work with Lisa and Natasha as new editors – thank you for your hard work and support for our authors and our values. Especial thanks for ensuring that disruption is at the heart of this book as we need it even more. We want this book to inspire waves of small and huge disruptions to the status quo for women in education, so let's all move forward purposely to disrupt, to innovate and to bring about the change we need.

Lisa's Acknowledgements

I want to acknowledge Cynthia Chambers. I don't know if she really understands the impact she had on me as I started my teacher journey. She introduced me to writing as recovery, for figuring things out and for connecting with others. I started finding my voice in her courses and haven't really shut up since! She has my gratitude.

Natasha's Acknowledgements

I would like to express my gratitude to my husband, Malchus, and my children, Kelese, Kayde, and Kaynan, for their patience as I immerse myself in my work, often focused on a screen. Additionally, I am deeply thankful for the incredible women who surround me, particularly the inspiring members of the WomenEd community. Your unwavering support and encouragement motivates me to persevere in this important work.

GET INVOLVED WITH WOMENED

We hope we have inspired you to engage with WomenEd, and to disrupt elements of the status quo so women are treated more equitably in education. One of the best ways to do this is to go to a WomenEd event. Events are posted on our website and shared on our social media sites. Our community is also full of prolific blog writers, so have a look at the blogs on our website to see the issues our community explores. Our current networks have their own pages on our website, so do join in with your country or regional activity.

Here are some ways you can contact and connect with us:

Website: womened.com

Email: womened@womened.com

X (formerly Twitter): @WomenEd is our main Twitter account. Our hashtag #WomenEd is used for events and networking so join in the conversation globally. Search for @WomenEd on Twitter and a list of our current networks appears.

Blue Sky: https://bsky.app/profile/womened.bsky.social

LinkedIn: www.linkedin.com/company/womened/

Facebook: www.facebook.com/womened

YouTube: www.youtube.com/channel/UC_pQlP0WTeKl7MDlDd0-9aA

Instagram: @womenleaders: www.instagram.com/womenedleaders

Newsletter: sign up at: https://72bfd75b.sibforms.com/serve/MUIFADC2P7GxbCP HBoTT4IpJa9bJz364x5-hDEGt4-3r8D3bhc2mhEvravNulJFhImSqQfa2tBnN_I04jn_ doWSur0wjGqzac8U7Z6yRmpk7qokCNlbqSGAmB5RBC6vTyDMjMYF0Znux- hk2IFmgL_epyCMKezf-_bvHg7HKDVZCTdm-rYhqzlRM9IkwwU0oU5Qz2MBGnNf- HgTcTJ

PART I

INCREASING THE REPRESENTATION OF WOMEN IN LEADERSHIP

INTRODUCTION

Lisa Hannay

As authors of our destiny, every decision is a sentence, every action a paragraph and every dream is a chapter waiting to be written ... so write ... #10%braver. (Islam, 2024)

In late September 2023 I travelled from Canada and spoke at the WomenEd global unconference in London. This annual event of disruptive women gathers voices from around the globe to challenge the status quo, spotlight women leaders and cultivate networks.

Rather brazenly, I insisted that 'they' didn't want us here at the unconference, didn't want us to gather or be emboldened and support one another. I stand by this statement.

Maya Angelou has said, 'Each time a woman stands up for herself, without knowing it, possibly without claiming it, she stands up for all women' (The Office of Hillary Rodham Clinton, 2007). Each day we put our feet on the earth is another day to push back, to disrupt, to challenge and to change the system.

They (white, conservative, straight, Christian, usually male) want us to remain in our place. To keep us in our place, they pay us less, enact healthcare laws that punish women for their biology and create working conditions that often make women choose between career and motherhood. They are both insidious and overt at keeping women in their place. Every time there is a gathering of women at a conference or workshop, or women grow a network on social media, or women write a chapter for a book, these disruptive women refuse to accept the notion that women should stay in their place. Indeed, these women disrupt this notion entirely, opting to create a place of their own.

In this section several authors disrupt the status quo simply by being 10% braver and submitting a chapter for this third WomenEd book. The authors highlight the importance of building supportive networks, using social media, speaking at and attending conferences, and blogging to build these networks. These networks support, challenge, push and disrupt old ways of thinking and being that have kept women in their supposed place. These networks grow confidence, challenge bias, and help women change behaviour that has kept them from pursuing leadership.

Breaking away from perfectionism, imposter syndrome, letting go of shame and guilt are all themes in this section. In Kiran Satti's chapter, Kiran challenges women to think about the unconscious bias that lives in the very fabric of our society. This bias keeps us from embracing who we are and divides us from who we are to who we think we must be to lead. Kiran uses Barbie and The Dream Gap Project to assert that women don't have to fit any mould to become leaders.

Other contributors, Amy Bowdler, Bianca Greenhalgh, Nasima Riazat, Jess Gosling, Jess Mahdavi-Gladwell, and Rebecca Hoyes all discuss networking, building confidence, and battling against unconscious bias and systemic barriers as they pursued leadership roles. None of their journeys were simple, nor were they asking or expecting leadership to be simple. Women are not asking for simple or different, they are asking for equitable leadership opportunities free from bias and barrier.

The chapters in this section are written by women who wouldn't stay in their place. In fact, these chapters are written by women who have a firm belief and commitment to the idea that all women belong in all places. Ruth Bader Ginsberg said, 'Women belong in all places where decisions are being made. It shouldn't be that women are the exception' (Mears, 2009). The authors in this section carved out their own place by confronting the bias that previously held them back, acknowledging the barriers that prevented them from pursuing leadership and looking for connection and community in professional learning networks, such as WomenEd. They teach us that women should and must be represented fully in leading education.

As you read, please consider what you will disrupt today and make it happen for you and all women.

(See: https://womened.com/representation-campaign)

References

Islam, S. [@WCA_education] (2024) 22 January [X] Available at: https://x.com/WCA_education/status/1749556564053090402?s=20 (accessed 25 January 2024).

Mears, B. (2009) 'Justice Ginsburg ready to welcome Sotomayor', *CNN Politics* [Online]. Available at: https://edition.cnn.com/2009/POLITICS/06/16/sotomayor.ginsburg/index.html (accessed 15 January 2024).

The Office of Hillary Rodham Clinton (2007) *Dr. Angelou announces endorsement of Clinton*. Previously available at: www.hillaryclinton.com/video/35.aspx.

1

TIME TO USE OUR SUPERPOWERS

Amy Bowdler

KEY POINTS

This chapter will:

- explain how I drew on my early experiences to drive future success
- explore ways in which I built the bridge to close my confidence gap
- encourage you to reflect upon where your own confidence gap began to help you unleash your superpowers as a woman.

Introduction

You've heard about the age gap, the gender pay gap, and the dreaded thigh gap noughties teenagers like me were bombarded with as the key to looking like, feeling like, and achieving success. For each of these, cultural and institutional influences have formed barriers to true female success. However, have you ever considered their significance in creating the confidence gap? This chapter will look at how to identify where yours began and how best to build your own bridge over it for future success.

Where Did It All Begin?

Reflecting when my confidence gap began to grow, I am distinctly drawn to three early memories. Firstly, my mother and grandmother telling me that, at a Year 2 primary school parent–teacher conference, the teacher said that I was not the most academic child and I would be very good at shop work. Secondly, not being selected to read lines in a school play because clever girls and boys were the ones who were great at such things. Thirdly, being told at a Christmas carol concert rehearsal that I would only be picked to sing a solo if I didn't get ridiculous and excited about it as I usually did.

It was from these moments I began to look inwards; self-doubt stirred up within and the beast began its gruelling quest towards imposter-syndrome city.

It has been in identifying and reflecting upon these early moments that I realise the significance of each one being uttered by a woman, one of whom went on to become a Headteacher. I often question, what were the moments in their own lives that had led them to this behaviour? What systematic barriers had they internalised and were now normalising in their own behaviour? Whatever they were, I am determined to ensure it is not repeated in my own actions.

Although significant progress has been made in disrupting systematic barriers, dozens of the accomplished women I have worked with have also been constrained by this inequitable force. The power of that elusive self-doubt is so crippling it has held them back from taking the next step, even when they are so capable and worthy of achieving. Sheryl Sandberg, former chief operating officer (COO) of Meta was once quoted: 'There are still days I wake up feeling like a fraud, not sure I should be where I am' (cited in Hannon, 2014). Identifying the root of the issue is essential if you are to understand how to build a bridge over your own confidence gap. These early moments can never be forgotten and therefore the gap can never be closed; it is a part of you which makes you who you are today. However, ultimately identifying, recognising, and deconstructing the origins could help you to work on hurtful patterns you have formed and lead to building a future which is not controlled by these early experiences.

Building the Bridge

Unfortunately, in these early experiences I was of an age in which I had no ability to challenge and disrupt these behaviours and barriers alone. Cue the Superwomen in my life: a girl with a mother and grandmother who simply would not accept such glass-ceiling-establishing words.

Shirley Chisholm, the first Black US Congresswoman, once said, 'If they don't give you a seat at the table, bring a folding chair' (Chisholm, 1972). I learned to take a chair to every table and thrived on the desire of my personal Superwoman to disrupt the norms and prove the early version of my world wrong. I was taught that if I was at the table (no matter who was there, whether I was invited, or if I carried my bags of enthusiasm), I would always make that little space in the world a better place. In my teenage years, I developed an extremely strong work ethic, and had a passion for new experiences. I thrived off learning, making it my personal responsibility to seek out new opportunities. I was determined to *challenge* the thoughts of my early world to demonstrate my capabilities. I drew from the strength and *confidence* my Superwomen had in me to lay the foundations of my own self-belief by slowly examining and defining what mattered most to me. I began to bridge the *confidence* gap within me.

Ironically, I learned as much about the importance of *communication, connection*, and *community* from my proud 4-year stint as a part-time supermarket shop worker as I did in gaining my first-class honours degree at university. The lack of these 'three Cs' in those early negative experiences planted the seeds of what grew to become my core values. Over my 10 years in teaching and education leadership, they have driven both personal growth and growth within the teams I have led. I have learned to build strong *connections* with others by *communicating* openly, honestly, and respectfully, with warmth and a sense of humour. This has enabled me to express my own thoughts, feelings, and needs more clearly and led me to understand the thoughts, feelings, and needs of others around me more successfully.

Perfectionism Pit Stop

With a drive and determination to prove the world wrong about gendered assumptions, perfectionism became a new hurdle for me early in my teaching career. Although my goals remained clear, I would not necessarily put myself forward for roles until I had more experience, believing that this would give me greater confidence and credence. This reflects the experience of many women – as Vivienne Porritt (2019) cites in the work of Kay and Shipman (2014), 'women don't consider themselves as ready for promotion … and they generally underestimate their abilities'.

Consequently, I quickly became frustrated as I watched older colleagues or seemingly more *confident* colleagues (many of whom were men) take on new roles and risks, so I checked in again at imposter-syndrome city. Luckily, a chance encounter with the WomenEd Twitter community, and taking part in their 'Inspiring Women Leaders' programme in 2019, quickly led me to question whether my colleagues were more competent or were they just more self-assured? This inspiring group of new superwomen spoke honestly and openly about what was possible, like my mother and grandmother had before. As Menah Pratt states, '… I want women and girls to feel empowered to discover and share their superpower with the world. Now more than ever, women's voices are needed worldwide' (Gasman, 2024). It is empowering to know that countries and states led by women saw one-sixth as many Covid-19 deaths during the early stages of the pandemic as those led by men and were projected to recover sooner from recession (Fioramonti et al., 2020: paragraph 3). Which superpowers did these women use?

As Laker (2021: paragraph 7) states, 'Porritt believes, while recognizing that correlation is not causation, the success of women leaders during the pandemic seems to stem from:

- participatory and inclusive leadership
- clear and strong communication
- learning from others
- transparency
- compassion, empathy, and honesty.'

It is more than time to review what a leader in education looks like and what we look for in a leader.

Time to Use My Superpower

I realised I had to take the leap of faith and ensure my voice and superpowers were used. It was time to check in with those values and goals once again to determine where to go next. My bridge of confidence has been built with bricks of competence, but its foundations lie within my values; it lies within acknowledging the size of my passion to make a difference in my little space of the world, to show what women like you and I can achieve. My reasons why are integral to my success: my passion for equity, my enthusiasm for my role, and my commitment to supporting my *community* with warmth towards the main goal. Kirova (2023) recognised that identifying your core values can 'lead to an augmented sense of purpose'. By reminding yourself of why it is important for you to do something, your willpower is strengthened and you are more likely to act assertively and *confidently* for what you believe in. You are more likely to *disrupt* what the systemic stereotypes try hard to mould for you.

Maintaining the Bridge

I can't say that my bridge still doesn't wobble from time to time. The passing of my beloved mother and the feeling of loss towards my dementia-burdened grandmother have notably affected me. I lost those significant female role models who would fly the flag and champion me towards the next step. However, through these difficult times, I have learned that my bridge is stronger than I thought. It is reinforced by the other women and men in my life who believe in me unwaveringly.

I have learned to ask the key question: If they believe in me, then why don't I?

My bridge is supported by the inspirational women in education I have had the pleasure of working with; those who build up others, not just themselves, and represent and support the *community* with warmth, respect and honesty in their roles as mentors.

Empowering others to build their own bridges and unfurl their own powers and potential is an incredibly important element of my own leadership and requires a greater level of skill. It is important to be a brave and honest mentor, who provides authentic support for other women to be represented at the table, to be someone who guides potential leaders towards long-lasting futures in such roles. This is something I continue to develop with success in my current role as a Deputy Headteacher at a primary school in the North East of England. I would love to share that with those teachers who began to build my confidence gap. I also support middle leaders with subject leadership and work within local authority groups to develop English subject leadership, a particular passion of mine.

As with any bridge, it's good to check in on those foundations which keep it sturdy. Once you've discovered what matters most to you, your personal powers, and you learn to draw upon them whenever you need to, your bridge will maintain its strength and continue to stand tall and proud with the support of your people. Don't wait around: it is always the right time to show the world what you can achieve. Be 10% braver in building that bridge over that *confidence gap*. Because if not now, when? And if not you in your dream role, then who?

Disruptions

- Never underestimate the value in taking the time to reflect upon which experiences have had the most significant impact upon you to this very day. What did they make you feel like and how have they contributed towards building your foundations? What is most important to you?
- Consider carefully how your values can be garnered for strength and to help you grow towards your goal.
- Find your people: seek out your *community* to build your bridge. Think who is within your network to provide the warmth and honesty you truly need to hear to reflect and move forward. There will be those you lean on for the different strands of your personal and professional life, and all are important in supporting you to build the bridge over your confidence gap and help you to disrupt the norms.
- Finally, think, where do my own strengths lie to support the bridges of others? It is no good merely skipping across your own bridge, while you watch others struggle behind you. Embracing negative experiences, checking in with them often, and being honest about your own story may just encourage another woman to take the first step towards closing their own confidence gap and to be someone else's superwoman.

References

Chisholm, S. (1972) 'About Shirley Chisholm', *A Seat At the Table* [Online]. Available at: www.bringyourownchair.org/about-shirley-chisholm/ (accessed 17 July 2023).

Fioramonti, L., Coscieme, L. and Trebeck, K. (2020) 'Women in power: It's a matter of life and death', *Social Europe*, 1 June [Online]. Available at: www.socialeurope.eu/women-in-power-its-a-matter-of-life-and-death (accessed 15 January 2024).

Gasman, M. (2024) 'To be fierce, fearless and to claim your superpower', *Forbes*, 22 January [Online]. Available at: www.forbes.com/sites/marybethgasman/2024/01/22/to-be-fierce-fearless-and-to-claim-your-superpower/ (accessed 23 January 2024).

Hannon, K. (2014) 'The no. 1 way women can succeed more at work', *Forbes*, 24 April [Online]. Available at: www.forbes.com/sites/nextavenue/2014/04/24/the-no-1-way-women-can-succeed-more-at-work/?sh=2561c534b17c (accessed 16 June 2023).

Kay, K. and Shipman, C. (2014) 'The confidence gap', *The Atlantic*, May [Online]. Available at: www.theatlantic.com/magazine/archive/2014/05/the-confidence-gap/359815/ (accessed 12 January 2024).

Kirova, D. (2023) 'What are core values, and why are they important?', *Values Institute*, 26 February [Online]. Available at: https://values.institute/what-are-core-values-and-why-are-they-important/ (accessed 17 July 2023).

Laker, B. (2021) 'We need to rethink strategic leadership', *Forbes*, 21 January [Online]. Available at: www.forbes.com/sites/benjaminlaker/2021/01/21/we-need-to-rethink-strategic-leadership/ (accessed 15 January 2024).

Porritt, V. (2019) 'What price equality?', in V. Porritt and K. Featherstone (eds), *10% Braver: Inspiring Women to Lead Education*. London: Sage.

2

POWERFUL STORIES

Bianca Greenhalgh

KEY POINTS

This chapter will:

- discuss increasing representation of women in leadership roles by exploring networking in the context of my own personal and professional journey at a point when education was about to lose another female leader
- explore vulnerability, perfectionism, and the power of narratives in keeping this leader in the 42% of female Headteachers in secondary schools
- help you harness the power of networking and draw on such power.

We Have Lift Off!

Phase one started on a *Women Leading with Confidence* course, with interview advice on making sure you wear your best underwear and don't wear heels if you normally wear flats! Then a hug from a stranger, asking 'Where do you live?' and 'Yes, WomenEd does need a Sussex lead, but you have to be on Twitter' (Porritt, personal communication, 29 November 2018).

Twitter??

Yes, Vivienne Porritt, you dragged me kicking and screaming into the world of Twitter. Those who know me would probably say I don't have an issue with confidence, so this would be easy, right? Well, yes, in many ways I had been privileged with transferable networking skills from my hospitality experience before my second career in education. My comfortable space was not always with women though, not large groups anyway. I was curious about the opportunity presented and the course was my intentional start, getting out there and learning from others in what was purported to be a safe space for women. It did not and has not disappointed.

To Be or Not …

Headship – my goal from the beginning of my educational career. I had been on a charmed journey: 17 years in education, with 9 years' senior leadership experience, honing my skills and progressing towards that goal. I projected I would be a Headteacher by 45 and started my first Headship in September 2020 and turned 45 two weeks later. Teaching is an incredibly rewarding profession, whilst stepping into leadership can have its challenges and Headship is hard. I don't think that anything ever prepares you for how isolating Headship can be; accountability, the safety of staff and children, shifting sands with policy, and more recently the impact Covid and lockdowns have had on the mental health of many. You only need to read about the Ruth Perry story (Connor, 2023; Sinmaz, 2023) to understand the weight of responsibility on Headteachers and how intrinsically linked to one's sense of identity it is and the impact that those accountability measures can have on individuals. At the time of writing this, 42% of Headteachers in state-funded secondary schools in England are female, and Black or other global majority groups sit at 2.6% (Gov.UK, 2023). Although slowly improving, this representation is still not good enough compared to the proportion of women in the education sector. As a woman and a Headteacher I was proud to be part of that statistic, representing women in leadership and creating spaces for others on their leadership journey.

After 18 months, for my own wellbeing, I stepped away from my Headship.

I wasn't sure what would be next, having spent so much of my career working towards this position. It took this moment in time, a significant change in my career and life, to realise asking for help and being vulnerable was not something to fear. I certainly think that recently, after the Ruth Perry story broke, more Headteachers have shared their narrative of how difficult it can be. At the time this was not the case, and I now know that telling our stories is one way to keep women in leadership. If we don't share our stories, leaders will continue to feel alone in the challenges they face, setting high expectations of themselves, working to do it all, without asking for help. 'Perfection is not attainable, but if we chase perfection, we can catch excellence' (Lombardi, n.d.) was a mantra I had used. During this time, through fear of failing to be perfect and with nothing to which I could compare my experiences, I was starting to wonder whether that confidence was real or a persona I had created in this pursuit.

The Art of Perfection

Discussing perfection, Brene Brown cites Nicholas Wilton's writing where he states that 'art is all just perfectly imperfect' (Brown, 2015: 136). The art of perfection I had created for myself hadn't prepared me for the challenges of Headship. I had set myself excessively high personal standards, and when I was amid Headship, it had significantly knocked that confident persona almost everyone knew. Charlotte Woolley (2020) discusses how girls internalise perfection, putting others first, whilst still striving for personal perfection. This is me, advising others, not taking my own advice, and internalising my recent experience, which, in that moment, felt like failure. I had read the books; I had worked hard at an ethical leadership approach and had become a Headteacher at the most challenging of times and in the latter months I thought I had shown my vulnerabilities. None of this felt imperfectly perfect. My response then became a belief that this vulnerable leadership business is nonsense.

Brown also shares that being vulnerable doesn't mean oversharing, something I am skilled at and which I learned the hard way. Ah, I had misunderstood what it was to be vulnerable! I wish I had read her book back then to give me the clarity I needed. Reflecting on this time, I know that I had leaned on certain colleagues more than I should have, which was unfair of me. However, what I learned from this is that it is good to find the right spaces to lean into. For me, in part, it was my WomenEd community who supported me by opening new opportunities, one of which was my presentation at Pedagoo Hampshire 2022 speaking about the gremlin that kicks in or kicks you in times of adversity.

Embracing the Gremlin Ninja Warrior

As I moved into phase two, my 'Gremlin Ninja Warrior Training' (Brown, 2015: 74) journey began. I had to get my best big girl pants on (not just for interviews) and get myself out there to work out what I wanted to do next and how I was going to get face to face with the connections I had made through my network, when I was at my most vulnerable. The first part of this was to review what was and was not in my control. I had made my decision; I had to own this and take control of what I did next and that was to put myself out there however scary it was. The importance of networking, I discovered, is the power of sharing narratives. Speaking at the WomenEd Global Unconference around the same time as Pedagoo Hampshire, I shaped my narrative, spoke my truth and because of this someone got in touch with me. We met face to face for the first time more recently. She said that I had shown my vulnerable self, which gave her hope, as she was going through her own, similar experiences. So, being vulnerable was not so bad after all if sharing my narrative in a welcoming environment gave someone else the hope that I had when others had shared their stories with me. There is something in the synergy of this I am excited to explore further.

Networking creates an energy of its own. 'Networking that's all about caring human relationships, rather than transactional assessments' (Ezekiel, 2023) is what will aid personal growth. Engaging with networks is like having access to many mentors. I do not mean that in a transactional way in its traditional sense. There is something in the reciprocity in networks that allows for people to give and take in support of their own personal and professional growth. The key is to be open to challenge, be curious and be ready to ask questions that 'move from "small talk" to "deep talk"' (Arscott, 2022) which will aid that growth. Thank those who have created space for you, overtly and by paying it forward and holding space for others. Place yourself in spaces where you are an energy giver and not an energy hoover as it places you in a better position for deeper and more meaningful connections that take you on new and interesting journeys. Do engage more fully in networking; social media is a useful tool for this and you will meet amazing individuals. Find spaces to volunteer, supporting others through these networks. There are many people I interact with whom I have not met and I have met others face to face, and the strength of these connections has reinstated my faith in women lifting and elevating women. In our societal systems women will often be pitched against women, breeding a culture of distrust. As women together, we are a powerful entity to disrupt the systems that limit us.

I have found a space where I am thriving career-wise, within a community of good people who want the best for children and support each other's learning and growth. I reflect on where I was when I was ready to leave education and now, as an Executive Headteacher, I am proud that I still contribute to the representation of women in Headship, maybe even adding to the marginal improvements. It has taken me a while to rebuild my confidence and I do have moments that trigger old feelings. However, I make sure that I check in with myself, draw on the support of my network, sit and work through feelings to recognise patterns before reframing and moving forward.

Yoko Ono (n.d.) said, 'Art is my life and my life is art'. I would go further to say that all life is art. As someone who started out in performing arts as a dancer, I found that I explored the ideas and philosophies I was exposed to through creating dance; a way of communicating my making sense of the world. If 'Art is perfectly imperfect' (Swanson, 2023), then life is also imperfectly perfect and that must work for us. The power of people together, supporting, championing, creating spaces for others' voices and lifting each other up is the most satisfying and nourishing activity in which anyone could be involved. Essential to personal and professional growth is a move from critical internal chatter to harnessing the power of networking and sharing the dance.

Disruptions

- In taking the next step, whatever it is, take the lessons you have learned to create opportunities. It might be useful to use a tool such as Stephen Covey's 'Circle of Control and Concern' (2004). It will help you to step out of the emotional response and help order your thoughts.
- Fear is an opportunity to face challenge. If you fear putting yourself out there, be 10% braver and do it anyway. You will be surprised how amazingly supportive other human beings are and you will make connections that will help you realise you are not alone in your experiences.
- Say yes to opportunities you don't think you are good enough for, because you are! Listen closely to the questions you are being asked, grow from them and act on them. You may inadvertently be asked why you are not doing something yet … think yes, why am I not doing this, and then work towards making it happen.

References

Arscott, C. H. (2022) 'A better approach to networking', *Harvard Business Review*, 29 November [Online]. Available at: https://hbr.org/2022/11/a-better-approach-to-networking (accessed 24th June 2023).

Brown, B. (2015) *Daring Greatly: How the Courage to be Vulnerable Transforms the Way We Live, Love, Parent and Lead*. New York: Penguin.

Connor, C. (2023) 'Ruth Perry: Prevention of future deaths report', *Courts and Tribunals Judiciary*, 12 December [Online]. Available at: www.judiciary.uk/prevention-of-future-death-reports/ruth-perry-prevention-of-future-deaths-report/#related_content (accessed 15 January 2023).

Covey, S. R. (2004) *The 7 Habits of Highly Effective People*. London: Simon and Schuster UK Ltd.

Ezekiel, E. [@eylanezekiel] (2023) 7 July [Twitter]. Available at: https://twitter.com/eylanezekiel/status/1677307731911356422 (accessed 7 July 2023).

Gov.UK (2023) *School workforce in England* [Online]. Available at: https://explore-education-statistics.service.gov.uk/find-statistics/school-workforce-in-england (accessed 10 September 2023).

Lombardi, V. (n.d.) 'Vince Lombardi quotes about excellence', *A–Z quotes* [Online]. Available at: www.azquotes.com/author/8997-Vince_Lombardi/tag/excellence (accessed 15 January 2023).

Ono, Y. (n.d.) *Goodreads*. Available at: www.goodreads.com/quotes/141219-art-is-my-life-and-my-life-is-art (accessed 15 January 2023).

Sinmaz, E. (2023) 'Headteacher killed herself after news of low Ofsted rating, says family', *The Guardian*, 17 March [Online]. Available at: www.theguardian.com/education/2023/mar/17/headteacher-killed-herself-after-news-of-low-ofsted-rating-family-says (accessed 10 September 2023).

Swanson, A. (2023) *Perfectly imperfect: The beauty of imperfection and authenticity in the creative process*. Available at: www.sweetpapayaarts.com/post/perfectly-imperfect-the-beauty-of-imperfection-and-authenticity-in-the-creative-process (accessed 15 January 2023).

Woolley, C. (2020) *The Lost Girls: Why a Feminist Revolution in Education Benefits Everyone*. Woodbridge: John Catt Educational.

3

HARNESSING THE POWER OF PROFESSIONAL LEARNING NETWORKS

Dr Jess Mahdavi-Gladwell

KEY POINTS

This chapter will:

- highlight the importance and value of Professional Learning Networks (PLNs) and how essential they can be at specific times and situations
- explore how all women in education can be enabled and encouraged to access PLNs
- examine how the value of PLNs can be emphasised, amplified and recognised
- explore how PLNs increase the representation of women in leadership roles.

Introduction

This book is for and about women leaders. It speaks of representation, diversity and flexibility, and considers how value and worth are reflected (or not) in pay. Effective and supportive professional networks relate to these connected themes and this chapter considers PLNs that I have been part of or seen on my journey. I believe that we should all have space and safety to be authentic and this sense of safety can be augmented by finding the right PLN. This chapter will give examples of the positive impact of PLNs to encourage everyone to seek them and trust them.

As we seek leadership tables where women are represented and diversity is present and valued, the power of genuine professional networks is immense. No one seeks inclusion based on a characteristic which they want to be perceived equitably. We don't want a job because we are (… insert protected characteristic here …), neither do we want a job or opportunity despite those characteristics. However, those seeking progression and development benefit from the knowledge, experience and connections within their networks to help, to support and to guide, and this is especially so for underrepresented groups in leadership which includes women.

When we think of diversity in leadership, there are examples of successful, connected leadership teams in education within and outside of school. The concept of diversity is broad and rich; to seek diversity of social and ethnic/racial background, to represent different genders and sexual identities, to share a table with those who have a disability or are at different stages of life and career is empowering. This empowerment can disrupt the inequitable status quo, and such disruption is vital when the status quo is the quiet insistence of a preponderance of white, male leaders, of imposter syndrome or the unyielding resistance of a glass (or concrete) ceiling. Tick-box compliance and tokenism, however, limit the positive diversification of teams. We may not, individually, be able to influence change quickly; however, together there are significant opportunities to effect change and progress at every point in our careers.

Professional Learning Networks and WomenEd Values

Women are frequently aware of the value of belonging and being part of something and the risks that come with being outside of everything. We seek community. Whether this is finding your place in school (the choir, a sports team, library crowd, those who audition for productions, etc.), finding others about to embark on a shared journey such as parenthood classes, connecting through a continuing professional development (CPD) event, or finding connection through enjoyment of a shared activity, PLNs offer a personal and professional community. However, in the work space,

> … from work-life balance to pay equity, when it comes to feeling known and being included, women consistently reported lower results than male respondents with respect to these belonging factors. Women were 25% less likely to say they felt comfortable sharing a dissenting opinion and were 20% less likely to say their unique background and identity were valued at their company. (Achievers, 2021)

The value of PLNs for women is that they offer belonging and advocacy that can be lacking in the workspace. Sometimes the outcomes are practical and built around collaboration, such as sharing knowledge or travelling to events together. Sometimes the outcome is connection – to not be, or feel, alone. Change can be daunting, particularly when clarity around our own values is needed. *Connection* and *communication* with others experienced in seeking or making the change you consider can bring courage and confidence.

When confidence is low and we are perhaps 'coasting', stuck, or avoiding things, networks can show care for our wellbeing. Where there is a trusting connection, our networks can also offer positive challenges by highlighting an issue or providing much-needed disruption to this state where growth and development are arrested.

How PLNs Helped Me to Be 10% Braver

At times I did need to look beyond my staffroom to find a network of peers. When the Chartered College of Teaching launched its Chartered Teacher programme (Chartered College of Teaching, n.d.), being part of the pilot cohort played a huge part in my progression. CTeach highlighted the value of our roles as teachers, leading to lifelong friends with whom I learned and reflected. My mentor challenged me to engage with Twitter, which became a gateway to networks including WomenEd. Regular contact with others from my cohort still provides me with continued support and encouragement.

My mentor also introduced me to *When the Adults Change* (Dix, 2017), which led to me being part of Teacher Hug Radio. Co-hosting a show, I became part of another network encompassing members of the Teacher Hug team and our guests who added to my understanding, providing challenge and onward connection with others.

When I moved outside of mainstream education, I found The National Organisation of Pupil Referral Units and Alternative Provision (PRUSAP), and through Sarah Johnson (PRUSAP Chair), I first wrote for *Schools Week*, and was invited to speak at a Westminster Insight conference which provided an excellent opportunity to network. Through Rachel Lofthouse, I joined another PLN as a CollectiveEd Fellow. An opportunity to take part in a Chain Reaction Conversation about hopefulness with others who also value coaching was a much needed opportunity to connect and reflect.

Once in a more senior role, I joined the WomenEd cohort of The National College of Education Senior Leadership Programme. I cannot overstate the importance of the amazing women in this PLN and our shared values. The course has ended, the connection will not. Groups including BAMEed allowed me to find further connection and to see small changes that I can make and seek within my spheres of influence. I learned about impactful action, especially in relation to anti-racism. Trusting Teachers, a network of Christian teachers and leaders in schools, has also been a PLN on which I lean.

These networks have fundamentally kept me working as an educator, especially one key conversation with Sam Twiselton, an Education expert, in March 2019. I was at a very low point in terms of professional self-belief. Sam's knowledge of my strengths, genuine care for me as an individual and her communication of both prompted a turning point; the conversation is one I revisit whenever I experience self-doubt. Every relationship which has supported me to develop as a teacher and as a leader arose from a network and from an 'us' story as described by Eastwood (2021) in his book *Belonging*.

I began a new role as a Deputy Head in a primary PRU in September 2023 and feel that I am representing women leaders and all the colleagues with whom I collaborate in my PLNs. Knowing how I have benefited from the PLNs I have experienced, I now seek to extend such opportunities for all women.

How Can All Women in Education Be Enabled to Access PLNs?

Our ability and capacity to interact with PLNs is impacted by other roles we fill, including caring and studying. Accessibility increases with the potential to meet others from home or work or online, to network across distance and time zones, and the option to engage when small children are in bed or while keeping an ear open for teenagers or elderly relatives. For some, in-person interaction after a day at work is overwhelming, but the option to join online, dipping in and out, is manageable. I've had positive experiences of in-person events at weekends and evenings. I was also able to attend the WomenEd 2022 Unconference online while needing to be at home to receive a rescheduled furniture delivery. I have been delighted when two events I've felt torn between (one about the links between knife crime and exclusion and one about flexible thinking) have both been online; not needing to travel between venues meant that I was able to attend both rather than choose only one. In the autumn of 2022, I was asked to present at a conference outside of the UK at relatively short notice. My responsibilities outside of work meant that being away for three days would have been practically difficult and emotionally stressful; being able to present online to delegates at an in-person event allowed me to contribute to the conference without feeling stressed about short-notice travel or that I was adding to the burden of others at work or at home. In *Being 10% Braver*, Penny Rabiger (2021: 163) reminds us that representation means providing 'a greater variety of voices and views', which may mean our PLNs need to ensure that women, especially underrepresented groups, are positively included by supporting with entry and travel costs to events.

How Can the Value of PLNs Be Emphasised, Amplified and Recognised?

Professional learning is career-long. Networking allows us to put a toe into the waters of potential, to find out more about a next step or change of direction from people with knowledge and desire to support. PLNs have value for teachers who are training, those early in their careers and for those considering and experiencing leadership. They also provide opportunity to reach behind and pull up the person behind us, to move beyond standing on the shoulders of giants (attributed to Newton, 1675) and offer a shoulder, or a leg-up, for someone else. Leadership may be perceived as a solitary journey, one where showing humanity or anything perceived as weakness has the potential to damage one's career trajectory. Personal Learning Networks can disrupt this perception, supporting the strengths of an individual and sharing knowledge and experience to support the learning needed to develop confidence and skills in areas where this is needed. Sharing and celebrating the impact of our experiences of PLNs and inviting others to belong can increase access to support and encouragement.

How Can PLNs Increase the Representation of Women in Leadership Roles?

To me, and the WomenEd community, as a women leader it is vital to lead authentically. One way to move towards this freedom to lead authentically is through strong connections with powerful women. It's through a palpable sense of those you respect believing in you. It's when someone who knows you well and deeply can explain your strengths and clarify how or why you are qualified and perfect for a role. It's when someone can be their authentic, hurt, bruised, triumphant, confused, learning self with another or others and those others can support and encourage development and progression.

I have seen the impact of women leaders 'reaching down to pull the next person up' (Porritt, 2023). I have benefited from the impact of networks in relation to building connections which can then be used to connect others, the second and third subsequent handshakes. I have seen a project inspired by WomenEd be followed by an increase in diversity in a Middle Leadership Team which is the beginning of a more diverse group of women progressing to more senior roles. I have seen PLNs support women to face up to and face down imposter syndrome.

I have seen PLNs within schools support the progression and professional success of women. I have also seen PLNs support the progression and professional success of women despite a negative environment within their school.

Let's all imagine high-performing, diverse women leaders being paid equitably, being free from the constraints and boundaries placed by others with no mandate to limit us. PLNs are an important way to support this goal.

Disruptions

- Find a Professional Learning Network that suits your needs so it will be experienced as supportive and useful.
- Use self-knowledge to reflect on whether face-to-face interactions drain or invigorate. Think about what you need and can commit to.
- Identify whether you need a network that overlaps with existing groups or one which is separate.
- Seek examples of when PLNs have helped others achieve your next step/longer-term goal.

- Ask yourself the difficult questions until you can discuss them with someone else. Coyle suggests four, including 'Is there something you've dreamed of doing for a long time? Why haven't you done it?' (Aron and Aron, 1997, cited in Coyle, 2018).
- Reach behind you, wherever you are on your journey, and help the next woman up.

References

Achievers (2021) *Women lag behind men on sense of belonging and feeling valued at work, new survey reveals* [Online]. Available at: www.achievers.com/press/women-lag-behind-men-on-sense-of-belonging-and-feeling-valued-at-work-new-survey-reveals/ (accessed 15 January 2024).

Chartered College of Teaching (n.d.) *Chartered status* [Online]. Available at: https://chartered.college/chartered/ (accessed 15 January 2024).

Coyle, D. (2018) *The Culture Code: The Secrets of Highly Successful Groups*. New York: Random House Business.

Dix, P. (2017) *When the Adults Change, Everything Changes: Seismic Shifts in School Behaviour*. Carmarthen: Crown House Publishing.

Eastwood, O. (2021) *Belonging: The Ancient Code of Togetherness*. London: Quercus Editions.

Porritt, V. (2023) Academy of Women's Leadership Conference presentation, 21 January.

Rabiger, P. (2021) 'We can't be what we can't see: Make sure you are not the one blocking the view', in K. Featherstone and V. Porritt (eds), *Being 10% Braver*. London: Sage/Corwin.

4

IMPOSTER SYNDROME

QUIETENING THE VOICES IN OUR HEADS

Jess Gosling

KEY POINTS

This chapter will:

- help you recognize that feeling like an imposter is not a medical syndrome, but part of the human condition and based on feelings, not facts
- provide examples of how to increase your confidence, and reduce feelings of self-doubt and criticism
- encourage you to network in areas outside of the workplace, as collaborating and building a community can support your personal development.

Introduction

When defining imposter syndrome, it is worthwhile to note that it is not a syndrome, with any medical credence. Instead, the term can be understood as feelings which have become so common, they have become part of, or the problem of, the human condition (Clifton, 2020; Hibberd, 2019).

An individual can feel like an imposter at any stage of their career, and in a range of contexts such as taking on a new job or project, or when changing workplaces or departments, or even when new staff are appointed at a current school.

Experiencing imposter syndrome can feel crippling, resulting in a lack of confidence, nerves, fear of failure, as well as perfectionism. The irony is that imposter syndrome particularly affects those who are successful and intelligent and have no obvious reason to feel insecure (Hibberd, 2019). Yet these individuals might not ever feel successful, no matter how they are perceived by others. They are likely to heavily self-criticize, are unable to accept compliments, and instead focus on where they are falling short (Hibberd, 2019).

In this chapter I recount some of my 'imposter' experiences. I overcame these experiences by being proactive; through developing a support network, creating boundaries for my work, enhancing my professional knowledge, and accepting that I do not need to be an expert in all that I do in order to be good at it. Being mindful and aware of your feelings will help you listen to the positive voices. Due to the gendered assumptions associated with the term, it is important we share our stories of this very human condition, alongside ways of overcoming it. If you let this feeling consume you, it will prevent you from achieving what you are capable of.

Unrealistic Expectations: The Need to Prove

Following an extended maternity leave, I started a new job in a fast-paced school, where I perceived my colleagues as far more capable than I. To keep up, I worked extremely hard and was permanently exhausted and deeply unhappy. I missed the time and energy I had previously with my daughter, and my ability to parent her how I wanted to. Feeling close to burnout, I felt unsuccessful at both teaching and parenting.

Following my first term, my Assistant Head told me that I'd given a strong lesson observation, that I was handling my role fantastically – so why was I still so hard on myself? I was struck dumb by this comment, as no one else had ever identified what I put myself through. She explained that giving 150 per cent every single day was not sustainable for anyone. I was striving for a level of perfection which could never be achieved.

I decided to change my expectations, but this was not easy. I followed Cognitive Behaviour Therapy (CBT) sessions and the therapist identified that I was terrified of making mistakes. I would have nightmares about this! For one week she challenged me to journal everything I did 'wrong' in the workplace, alongside any praise I received. At the end of the week, the section on wrongdoings was blank.

Such worries are a common feeling for those with imposter syndrome, whereby the individual has feelings which are in no way based in truth (Hibberd, 2019). By constantly anticipating disapproval or criticism, I was working in a frantic state and limiting my ability to enjoy my life outside of work. I effectively reduced the experiences with my daughter, which ultimately mattered the most to me.

Therefore, I began to intentionally change how I worked, first by setting boundaries. I left my classroom for morning break two times per week, then three times and so on. I would only work for a certain amount of time in my lunch hour. I recognized that being perfect was unachievable, and that, in fact, my good was good enough. This change in mindset has helped me to be much better at recognizing any unrealistic expectations.

Feeling Out of Depth When Exploring Something New

WomenEd argues that, to tackle the barriers women leaders face, and to develop and grow, we need to be 10% braver and try new experiences. However, we can underestimate how challenging inexperience can be. If you are not prepared to accept that you have much to learn in a new role, then this can also feed into the imposter feeling.

When I found out that I would return to teaching in the Early Years, I was ecstatic. However, despite postgraduate study in this area, I had had a substantial time period away from teaching this age range. I became anxious, as I felt I had so much to learn.

My line manager was an empowering leader, so she encouraged me to take on projects to support the team and develop our environment. I listened intently to my colleagues and reflected on their work as well as my own. Through active listening and learning, I became secure in pedagogy. I remember one parent quizzed me on play-based learning and I rose to the challenge fielding his questions expertly. I sought professional development and wrote about classroom experiences, and my articles gained recognition in the field. I waited for someone to contest my work, or argue it, but this never came. I innovated a new way of working to support our students, which was well received. This intense period of learning and sharing my discoveries was my way of proving I was good enough, but also helped me overcome my self-doubt.

I went on to author a guide on international teaching, and whenever I put myself forward to publications, almost all my ideas were accepted. However, I did not perceive myself as doing anything special or out of the ordinary, believing that 'When you do well, which you almost always do, you tell yourself anyone could have done it' (Hibberd, 2019: 9).

Yet a new world began to open to me as my articles and blogs were shared across social media platforms. The support I received disrupted my self-perception and led to further personal development. Scrolling one day through my Twitter feed, I was lucky enough to chance upon WomenEd.

Find Your Cause: Develop Your Self-Belief

By following WomenEd on Twitter, I could see that the organization was built through collaboration and empowerment, providing a voice to female leaders. Whilst in school, a member of staff approached me to discuss how she could progress in her career. I talked to her about how amazing she was in her role, and I remember she was tearful, as no one had said this to her before. I began to reflect on what I could do to support those working in education, at all levels, in my host country. Listening to someone with greater self-doubt than myself gave me the strength to help her and others. I had to put my own issues behind me. I sent a tentative message to WomenEd about the idea of creating a regional branch in Taiwan.

Natasha Hilton promptly replied to my message and I was encouraged to build a team to collaborate on running WomenEd Taiwan. I contacted two individuals, one of whom – Jessica Wang Simula – was not an educator but head of the PTA and central to the community. She told me she would never have considered working in the role had it not been for my passion and ability to convince her that this was the right thing to do. The other, Jaya Hiranandani, was an inspiring educator at my school and our values crossed beautifully.

Following the initial orientation with WomenEd, we committed to our first event. In this event I presented the core values and several female leaders shared their story. The group of women who attended wrote notes and hung on to our words, and it was clear that they needed this community. This new community was special, warm and kind. Such a group was innovative in Taiwan, as this was the first of its kind where multinational women were provided a caring environment in which they could share their voices. Following this event I co-hosted several more events, online and in person. I began to grow confident in my worth and appreciate all the amazing supporters of the WomenEd vision. I see myself as quiet and communal and may not fit the mould of how strong women look and sound. Yet our strength comes from anger when faced with bias and discrimination, and from the support of a global community of women who support and elevate us.

It is time for all of us to disrupt what we may believe about being a strong woman, as strength doesn't always present itself as those who speak the loudest or share their opinions the most forcefully. In fact, such role models are often represented by male leadership, which is something we should not feel we need to emulate. I realized by attending WomenEd events that it was often the most humble, authentic, quiet speakers that I tuned in to. Different women will respond better to voices to which they can relate. I believe a strong woman is authentic, articulate and passionate about her views and willing to share them, justifying and evidencing her beliefs.

Overcoming Feelings of Self-Doubt

To overcome feelings of self-doubt, I made changes to my mindset both personally and professionally. I left an environment where I no longer felt supported and the actions of others fed into my insecurities. In addition, I improved my knowledge through professional development, not only as a consumer but also as a producer. I networked with others in the field, receiving validation on my ideas and improving my self-worth as I became recognized as a strong practitioner. I also said 'yes' much more. I would agree willingly to experiences that threw me out of my comfort zone. I didn't listen to the inner monologue and effectively closed negative voices. My learnt behaviour of being self-critical would not have a place in my life anymore. Instead, I established a way to accept myself, which helped me to change and re-learn a new internal dialogue that to date has served me better (Clifton, 2020). To reflect the words of Eruteya, we are not an imposter, we are all 'pretty amazing' (2022).

By being 10% braver I put myself forward to be a guest on podcasts, which led to my being offered my own radio show. I was contacted by professional development providers as an expert in my field. It was suggested I put myself forward for the Fellowship at the Chartered College of Teaching, which I obtained. Through positive responses, I received confirmation that I am good enough, and I believe it! Moreover, I regularly remind myself that, if I am unable to internalize any of my successes, my view of myself cannot change (Hibberd, 2019).

To help yourself tackle any imposter feelings, also watch the brilliant Commencement Speech by Reshma Saujani (2023).

> People ask me all the time: how do I overcome #ImposterSyndrome? And honestly, I'm done answering that question. Because here's the thing: imposter syndrome isn't a syndrome at all — it's a scheme.

I think this will dispel any lingering feeling of not being worthy to lead and spark the way we need to disrupt the gendered stereotypes we have been fed which restrict and limit us.

Reframing: Moving Forward

Smith (2022) explains that reframing is when you allow yourself to consider reinterpreting a situation in a way that is going to help you move through it. We can move towards a fearful situation with intention.

I am now a middle manager and delighted to fully represent women leaders across education. It is fine that it is still fear-inducing for me as I have limited experience. I understand that no one starts a job knowing everything there is to know about it, but this won't stop me feeling insecure when I make a mistake. Yet, to break the imposter cycle I know it is important to push past my comfort zone (Hibberd, 2019). I will reframe this feeling to accept that mistakes will happen, but these errors will reduce as I gain experience and are, in fact, a sign of being human (Hibberd, 2019). As I tell my students, we learn best from mistakes!

As I transition from being an excellent teacher to a novice leader, I can now accept this will be a steep learning curve which I will survive with a little help from my friends.

Disruptions

- Analyse your environment, colleagues and networks. Do they support you or make you feel like an imposter? If they make you feel like an imposter, move on!
- Be authentic. We need role models who are truly diverse. Your voice will resonate with others' so make sure it is heard.
- Instead of trying hard to appear perfect in a new role, ask for support and guidance. Understand that we all need to start somewhere.

References

Clifton, R. (2020) *Love Your Imposter: Be Your Best Self, Flaws and All*. London: Kogan Page Limited.

Eruteya, K. (2022) 'You're not an imposter. You're actually pretty amazing', *Harvard Business Review*, 3 January [Online]. Available at: https://hbr.org/2022/01/youre-not-an-imposter-youre-actually-pretty-amazing (accessed 15 January 2024).

Hibberd, J. (2019) *The Imposter Core: How to Stop Feeling like a Fraud and Escape the Mind-trap of Imposter Syndrome*. London: Aster.

Saujani, R. (2023) 'Imposter syndrome is modern-day bicycle face', *YouTube* [Online]. Available at: www.youtube.com/watch?v=zMRcWj_GKxY (accessed 15 January 2024).

Smith, J. (2022) *Why Has Nobody Told Me This Before?* London: Penguin Books.

5

NETWORKING TO DEVELOP AND INNOVATE

Nasima Riazat

KEY POINTS

This chapter will:

- explore why meaningful networking is more than collecting potentially useful contacts
- share what actively curating a meaningful network looks like for women educators
- discuss how to mobilise networks to bring about equitable change.

Introduction

Consider the following:

- Who do you consider as part of your current network?
- How have you used your network so far to develop personally and professionally?
- On honest reflection, in what way is your network supporting you?

The WomenEd global community is organised around networks which 'bring about change, to innovate and to support and empower women to lead education' (Porritt et al., 2022).

The way we network is quite different from the stereotypical male world of networking. To many women, the '"old-boy network" – an informal system of connections through which men use their positions of influence to help other men' (Castrillon, 2019: para 1) – is a complete anathema. WomenEd networks draw on social network theory (Van der Baan et al., 2014: 5), so we are structured:

- for learning and relationships
- to create virtual and physical links
- to ensure clear functions that network activities serve for their community.

We believe that networking the WomenEd way is about drawing on one of our super-powers, which is developing a strong, female support group. The global WomenEd community has an amazing support group of 50,000+ women. Now that is a network!

WomenEd has eight values that drive our networks and the way we interact with the education community. Through the lens of the '8Cs', let's explore what meaningful networking looks like, and illuminate how we can draw on your own personal/professional learning network to work towards and achieve your professional and personal goals:

- Clarity: acknowledge the gender imbalance in education leadership
- Communication: actively seek to promote the WomenEd mission
- Connection: connect existing and aspiring leaders and those who support them
- Confidence: take opportunities to be #10%braver
- Collaboration: enhance collaboration and sharing of experience
- Community: create an inclusive and interactive community
- Challenge: highlight systemic barriers to more inclusive and diverse leadership
- Change: Collate evidence of impact on developing inclusive/diverse leadership.

Clarity

As a working definition, networking is engaging in specific behaviours where the aim is to pull together, cultivate and gain support from our personal contacts (Gibson et al., 2014). On a more personal level, networking may be summed up as not *what* you know, but *who* you know. I can probably attribute my successes to harnessing the power of my networks, rather than to my research, roles, or accomplishments. My network is a resource of colleagues to tap into freely when needed and reciprocate when required.

In my own school setting and academic work, I learned the heart of good networking is being able to build a circle of connections with others, staying connected, and knowing who could help me or others in my network. This triple balancing act is so much easier said than done!

Although the development of social media networks (such as Twitter, Facebook, LinkedIn, and Instagram) and face-to-face opportunities has made it easier to widen our circles nationally and internationally, it can still be a daunting task, and 'women generally hesitate to ask for what they want out of a networking interaction. Instead, they think about what they can do for the other person first' (Castrillon, 2019: paragraph 3).

I see some people networking effortlessly, yet others struggle to maintain the basics of networking and confuse it with friendship. When it comes to quality networking, where do you even begin?

Let me share with you my networking experiences, lessons learnt along the way and how I stay connected with my networks while holding down a busy day job and balancing family commitments and academic life. I hope it inspires and illuminates a way forward for you.

Communication

One of the reasons I was wary of networking was the lack of opportunity to connect with people outside of my immediate circle. Networking needed to be a safe positive experience which resulted in some level of exchange of experience, inspiration, or knowledge.

Attending face-to-face events during a busy school year was not a cost- or time-effective option. I felt I needed to be a charismatic communicator to have people interested in me and want to network with me. Did I really have the time and effort to expend in building my network? I wanted to strike a balance between not neglecting my network and not becoming known for constantly badgering people.

My network has developed substantially through social media, mainly Twitter and the development of my #phdchat thread and WomenEd. Different communication skills are needed for face-to-face events and for social media. For me, it's so much easier to send someone a tweet than it is to approach them in person.

As I began looking out for opportunities, I took advantage of attending events. I came across WomenEd, a grassroots organisation that initially started building its network on Twitter. A good place to start building your network is through following WomenEd on social media and following your regional WomenEd network as shown on the website (womened.com, n.d.). Consider writing for the WomenEd blog and attend and support local and national WomenEd events and Unconferences.

My first WomenEd event in Manchester, England and a BAMEed event in Bolton, England encouraged me to test the waters and network outside of my immediate circle. It is important to connect with as many people as you can within a short period of time, show interest in them and allow them to remember you. I realised I needed to express my priorities and interests but, at the same time, be aware that not everyone wants to add to their network. Networking should never focus on what others can do for you; it should always be a two-way street. What can you do for them by listening and offering help when you can?

Practical tips

- Rehearse some conversation openers
- Practise listening
- Manage your nervousness

- Control emotions
- Look how they are responding to you with verbal and non-verbal cues
- Smile!

It works well to have different networks to tap into for various parts of your life. I have a separate network for academia, as I do for the subjects I teach and those who can support me with my next steps career-wise. Active networking is a two-way process; both sides must be open to it and this means being clear about why you are building this link with this person or group.

Connection

Keeping a professional distance and allowing people to respond when they can, rather than immediately, is much easier for me. Explore who follows your local, national, and international WomenEd networks and connect with current and aspiring women leaders. Be aware of the difference between personal social media accounts to share your personal news with family and friends, and a professional account. A professional account would generally not contain anything you would not wish to share with your colleagues. In support of fully representing women leaders, remember to curate your networks to ensure you engage with and hear diverse voices and views.

Other low-cost ways to access resources, support, innovative ideas, opportunities, referrals, and introductions are LinkedIn and word-of-mouth recommendations. Consider attending WomenEd events and Unconferences to develop new friendships and be 10%braver by reaching out to women you do not know or who are not already in your circle or are from marginalised groups.

Look up, down, sideways, and around when building your network; for example, parents, recruitment companies, professional services, previous colleagues, other local schools, and word of mouth. The benefits of building connections with other professionals are numerous: stronger reputation, visibility, grassroots network to support you, improved connections and professional growth as your work and confidence improves.

Maintain good terms with everyone – today's social media conversation could be taking place with tomorrow's colleague!

Confidence

A good network can give you a boost with your career plans and personal goals. It can become a trusted place to silence that critical voice in your head, a place where you can start to feel you can go ahead with your plans.

When we feel self-confident, we are more likely to move forward with opportunities than unconsciously move away from them. Acknowledge your strengths and talents, set realistic goals and practise positive self-talk. A good way to start is to be available and actively add people to your network; let people feel comfortable approaching you with their ideas. Look to see what you can offer before making requests to take from others. What can they do for you in return?

Take the risks others avoid; inaction breeds fear and negativity. If things don't work out this time, have the confidence to try again with a different opportunity.

Collaboration

A good network can increase your knowledge base and help with access to resources and solve issues in more depth than if you work on them on your own. As educators, we are often great collaborators as we need to keep on top of our practice, be up to date and highlight things to work on together.

Use your network in various ways:

- to brainstorm new ideas
- to reach consensus on an issue where you feel conflicted or there are many options available
- analysing problems and finding solutions
- simply an ear to listen or a safe space to air your thoughts
- owning up to errors to someone unconnected with the original scenario
- articulating thoughts before you approach others.

At the heart of good collaboration is being open minded. Giving and receiving feedback is a two-way process. You feel stronger as you don't need to handle things on your own if there is a feeling of trust, reciprocity, and communication. The reward for curating an effective network is greater motivation, feeling less tired and getting better results.

Community

We may use the terms network and community interchangeably, but there is a difference between a community and a network. A community cares for people and has an identity (for example, WomenEd), whereas networks specifically connect people, opportunities, and resources at a smaller level. You belong to a community holistically, but a network belongs to you alone, and you are in control of who is part of it at any given time.

Networks are often much larger, whereas communities are smaller and more intimate. Communities tend to be part of a larger network, but not all networks are considered communities, and we have geographically global branches of WomenEd. A network is a group you want to be connected to, and it is also a community of people who want to be connected to you too. The larger WomenEd social media network helps you to grow and challenge, and the specific local and regional community networks support and elevate you.

Joining your regional WomenEd networks can help you build a community and begin to address the wellbeing issue.

Challenge

With hindsight, I wish I had planned beforehand about networking rather than just listening to speakers as getting to events takes time and money.

With no formal introductions during the 'free time', I felt reluctant to talk to others even though they were welcoming due to feeling my intentions may be misunderstood and people may dislike it. In a mixed session, 'Women (may) also tend to avoid networking with men in social settings because they don't want their behavior to be misconstrued' (Castrillon, 2019: paragraph 2).

Curating a network takes time and effort; don't be afraid to take the first step to make contacts. Remember to follow up your connection and keep in contact afterwards with a follow up direct message on Twitter, an email, or a quick tweet to show you have connected with them.

Change

A carefully crafted network may be effective in bringing about change in your professional life. Initially, this may be as simple as retweeting posts on Twitter. Remember, it is better to focus on quality over quantity of followers and curate a small, meaningful network initially. Post some engaging content on your own social media pages and practise good etiquette. It is easy to get drawn into conversations and strong opinions on social media, so decide which posts you wish to engage with and which are best just read.

Networking is a learning experience, so do not be put off if the early attempts seem slow and take a lot of effort. It takes time for the benefits of networking to be seen or felt and initially you may be offering support to others before you feel able to ask for any support for yourself.

Take a moment to reflect on what changes specifically you would like to make and then explore who may be useful to connect with to help make the change. How will you let people know what change you are considering? How can they help you? Most importantly, how can you and your network ensure increased representation of women leaders in education and how will you disrupt the inequitable status quo for women leaders?

Disruptions

- Use your network to bring about change, to disrupt the status quo and make a difference to women leaders now and in the future.
- WomenEd campaign to tackle inequality for women leaders in education by addressing the gender pay gap, encouraging flexible working, increasing representation of women in leadership roles, and increasing the diversity of

women in leadership positions. Choose one action from the website to aid these campaigns and work with your network to put it into practice.

- Networks of women have achieved equitable and social change throughout history and WomenEd are proud to learn from these women. Commit to the change you want to achieve and disrupt the current practice.

References

Castrillon, C. (2019) 'Why women need to network differently than men to get ahead', *Forbes*, 10 March [Online]. Available at: www.forbes.com/sites/carolinecastrillon/2019/03/10/why-women-need-to-network-differently-than-men-to-get-ahead/ (accessed 15 January 2024).

Gibson, C., Hardy, J. H. and Buckley, M. R. (2014) 'Understanding the role of networking in organizations', *Career Development International*, 19, 146–161.

Porritt, V., Free, L. and Hannay, L. (2022) 'Disruptors, innovators, changemakers', in G. Handscomb and C. Brown, *The Power of Professional Learning Networks*. Woodbridge: John Catt.

Van der Baan, A., De Haan, M. and Leander, K. (2014) 'Learning through network interaction: The potential of ego-networks', in V. Hodgson, M. De Laat, D. Mcconnell and T. Ryberg (eds), *The Design, Experience and Practice of Networked Learning*. New York: Springer, pp. 225–240.

WomenEd (n.d.) *Networks* [Online]. Available at: https://womened.com/networks (accessed 15 January 2024).

6

DISRUPTING SOCIAL NORMS

THE DREAM GAP PROJECT

Kiran Satti

KEY POINTS

This chapter will:

- explore owning our story, past, present, and future
- re-imagine representation of women leaders
- redefine the language of leadership.

Introduction

What would leadership mean to a 5-year-old girl? Maybe she hasn't heard the word or understood the concept? Does she have leadership role models and, if so, who are they? When she is 10 years old, does that understanding deepen or dissolve? Is her leadership potential being nurtured or hindered? What language is used to describe her? Is she assertive or bossy, emotional or compassionate?

Leadership is a skill, which is not gender specific; however, leadership has traditionally been defined as a masculine trait. In his *Harvard Business Review* article, Tomas Chamorro-Premuzic offers 'three popular explanations for the clear under-representation of women in management' (2013: para 1). He argues that aligning leadership to traditionally masculine behaviours has led to a climate where men (regardless of competency) progress due to a lack of barriers, whereas women must overcome many barriers, characterised by glass ceilings and concrete walls, irrespective of competency.

Enter the *Barbie* movie (2023).

Margot Robbie's iteration of the doll states, 'Barbie is a doctor, and a lawyer, and so much more ...'. This disrupts the perception that Barbie is objectified, commodified and stereotypical Barbie, as the idea is more than her appearance – she is possibility and potential. This sentiment is the underlying premise of The Dream Gap Project (Mattel, 2019), a global mission driven by Mattel to enable young girls to reach their full potential by actively dismantling the inequitable systems that are still in place today. Their research suggests that, even though girls believe in their potential, societal and gendered biases can impact a girl's future choices, which may hinder her fulfilling her full and future potential – whatever that may be, including becoming a leader. 'Barbie is all these women. And all these women are Barbie' (*Barbie*, 2023). This is Barbie's superpower, an idea that embodies possibility and potential, and encompasses anything and everything a woman can be.

My Origin Story

My Mum is my shero. She dismantled the cultural and societal narratives that would have enclosed all three of us (my mum, sister, and I) in a cage of disempowerment with no agency and no prospects. My Mum prevented the Dream Gap (Mattel, 2019) from becoming a barrier for her daughters (and in time, herself) because she valued us as humans and saw education as the bridge between our dreams and achievements. Being girls did not make either of us any less of a human and it was our human right to fulfil our potential in the world.

Fast-forward to my third year of teaching, successfully completing my Master's (whilst working) and just having taught in Tanzania over the Summer. An opportunity came up to apply for the English Lead post. I was shot down straightaway because it was perceived I couldn't be ready for such a role. My Dream Gap started in my early career and in my early twenties. I lost all belief that I could be a leader.

During my first five years of teaching, a specific type of narrative manifested itself:

- you're too small
- you're too pretty
- you're not white
- you're not ready to lead English
- you need to be more resilient
- you're too kind
- if you weren't so kind, I would not like you.

This narrative was limiting, along with very problematic representations of the women in leadership I was encountering which further solidified my belief that I couldn't be a leader, I didn't fit the mould. I began limiting myself because of the restricting beliefs associated with femininity. Considering my Mum had fought so hard in many ways for her girls to achieve, the world – ironically, the educational world – was telling me I wasn't capable of my potential because I was too feminine.

However, this mirrors the aims of Mattel's Dream Gap Project. Barbie is a stereotypical representation of femininity, and, to a certain degree, so am I. However, this should not determine anything about girls or women – it is unfair, biased and limiting – but it is the norm. A recent report by *The Guardian* shared the findings of the UN Development Programme which found, 'While there has been some progress ... social norms continue to be deeply entrenched and pervasive' (Ahmed, 2023). So, the societal and cultural norms that enable systems to undermine women's value and rights continue to be reinforced. Some of the most striking findings illustrated how pervasive prejudicial beliefs are:

- half of the people in 80 countries believe men make better political leaders
- 40% believe men are better business executives
- 25% believe it is justified for men to physically assault their wives.

The further impact of these findings stated that even though women are highly skilled and educated, there is still a 39% gender pay gap between men and women. When coupled with the above findings, which suggest that women's human rights inside and outside the workplace are undervalued and threatened, the picture is bleak.

For those who have seen the *Barbie* movie (2023), it encapsulates many societal biases and questions them at the same time. It's an invitation to re-imagine and take agency. Power is not finite and formidable. Power can be feminine and kind.

Gendered assertions about women and leadership are our kryptonite. So, how do we disrupt these assertions, biases and perceived norms that limit the possibility for us to realise and be represented as leaders, and to create legacy through change? Most importantly, how can we ensure the next generation of young girls and women do not have to smash through the glass and break through concrete ceilings to seize their potential roles as leading women of the future?

Reimagining Representation
The Disney Princess archetype

Reimagining the perception of the princess archetype is instrumental because it is one of the first representations of womanhood, femininity and gender that young girls (and, significantly, boys) encounter. Disney Princesses are deeply woven into the fabric of social consciousness. So how do we reimagine this visual representation of femininity becoming less of a damsel in distress and more of an agent of our own destiny? We need to take the lead and exercise our agency by reimagining the potential of a princess!

In *Defense of the Princess*, Jerramy Fine defines a princess as a queen in the making, 'A girl with vision and purpose higher than her own – she is characterised by her own agency, decision making and courage' (2016: 21). Muir (2022: paragraph 13) develops this potential further, stating that the representation of a princess has evolved, and she identifies different interpretations of a Disney Princess and femininity, dependent on the cultural context. In her research, it is evident that 'the depictions of the princess [have] changed over time' and so certain images of princesses were identifiable as role models. Therefore, we can assert with some hope that the projections of gendered roles are shifting (in popular culture, at least), which means we must consider that cultural and societal perceptions around gender are shifting too and have the potential to continue to evolve.

Take, for instance, the word pretty, a very feminine, commercialised concept. *Strong is the New Pretty* (Parker, 2017) is a good example of re-imagining pretty and its connotations. *Strong is the New Pretty* is a celebration of girlhood by broadening the scope, spheres and spaces girls can take up; it diminishes gendered binaries by diversifying the portrayal of girls and young women as active agents pursuing their dreams and interests.

This idea echoes how Barbie has been reimagined to represent over 250 careers, over 100 role models and a plethora of Science, Technology, Engineering and Mathematics (STEM) activities and initiatives. Barbie is all these women and all these women are Barbie.

The princesses in the Disney films, *Pocahontas* (1995), *Mulan* (1998, 2020), *The Princess and the Frog* (2009), *Tangled* (2010), *Brave* (2012), *Moana* (2016), *Frozen* (2013, 2019) and *Raya and the Last Dragon* (2021) are all re-imaginings of femininity and the princess archetype. They represent a spectrum of characteristics and take agency and create their own happy endings. Marriage as the happily ever after does not drive the plot; instead their dreams, purpose and agency do. This idea is echoed in Barbie's story and her story does not centre around being with Ken; she doesn't know what her happy ending is and that's fine. Though it could be seen as 'ironic given the feminist message of the film' that Ryan Gosling was nominated for an Oscar for playing Ken and Margot Robbie, as Barbie, was not (Glover, 2024)!

One of Ngozi Adichie's 15 suggestions from her *Feminist Manifesto* is to 'Never speak of marriage as an achievement' to your daughters (2017: 30). This is the reimagining that will help break down the societal biases and limitations placed on young girls and women.

The Disney/Marvel characters, such as Ms Marvel (a South Asian, Muslim), Shuri (a STEM icon) and Black Widow, represent a call to arms, agency and sisterhood. They are the reimagined representations of femininity and leadership taking ownership on our screens. This is inspiring. So how do we harness that potential in the real world?

Redefining the Language of Leadership

In the real world, we have WomenEd.

The sequel to my origin story starts with my path meeting several inspirational leaders from the WomenEd community who completely re-wrote my perception of leadership. They were smashing the mould, redefining the language, and creating spaces for women like me to not only *believe* I could be a leader but *could* become a leader. Within the six years of being part of WomenEd, I became a Senior Assistant Principal, English Leader, and Primary Trust Literacy Lead Practitioner. I've also written chapters for several education books and spoken at several educational conferences, including universities. I realised my superpower was using my voice. WomenEd disrupted the traditional, masculine narrative of leadership and empowered me to question and ultimately redefine my language of leadership.

Developing a language of leadership must start with questioning language first. The sixth suggestion from Ngozi Adichie's *Feminist Manifesto* is to question language because, 'Language is the repository of our prejudices, our beliefs, our assumptions' (2017: 26). Taking ownership of the language is a powerful way to dismantle the systemic biases and prejudices that undermine any progress towards fairness.

One belief that is beautifully blown up in Barbie Land, which Kelly (2023) highlights, is the idea that women owe their success to others, and therefore are 'internalising the disempowerment misogyny' that patriarchy has created. Kelly's article captures the fact that women should lean into their femininity, they should hold powerful positions, and they most certainly should take ownership in representing their achievements, harnessing their power through their voices and the language they choose to own their successes.

Broadening the language of leadership so that it is intersectional, inclusive and counter to the perceived norms, invites us, as girls and women, to take up our agency and draw our own box, cultivating our authenticity (Leese and Barker, 2022). Sandberg and Barksdale (2023) argue further that developing a 'more expansive definition of leadership' will enable young girls and women to view themselves as leaders and change agents. Within this expansion of leadership, it is crucial that terms like bossy and emotional are not leadership labels girls should fear. Instead, it's important we unmask the inequities and enable girls to question them. By questioning inequity, we are challenging, and ultimately disrupting it. Challenging inequity is brave, resilient and confident and these are leadership traits of the future. These are the superpowers we must nurture young girls to see in themselves, to own and to shine.

Disruptions

- Actively re-imagine role models, seek out role models that disrupt and dismantle the traditional, masculine concepts of leadership.
- Redefine language and leadership. Actively challenge and question biased terms towards women in leadership, like bossy, difficult or emotional.
- Join and support initiatives that enable girls and young women to discover and nurture their leadership potential, such as: The Barbie Dream Gap Project, https://girlsleadership.org/, https://inspiring-girls.com/ and Lean In Girls.

References

Adichie, N. C. (2017) *Dear Ijeawele, or a Feminist Manifesto in Fifteen Suggestions*. London: Fourth Estate.

Ahmed, K. (2023) 'Nine out of 10 people are biased against women says alarming UN Report', *The Guardian*, 12 June [Online]. Available at: www.theguardian.com/global-development/2023/jun/12/nine-out-of-10-people-are-biased-against-women-says-alarming-un-report (accessed 1 August 2023).

Barbie (2023) Directed by G. Gerwig [Film]. Warner Bros.

Chamorro-Premuzic, T. (2013) 'Why do so many incompetent men become leaders?', *Harvard Business Review*, 22 August [Online]. Available at: https://hbr.org/2013/08/why-do-so-many-incompetent-men (accessed 15 January 2023).

Fine, J. (2016) *In Defense of the Princess*. Philadelphia, PA: Runing Press.

Glover, A. (2024) 'Everyone's saying the same thing about Ryan Gosling's Oscar nomination', *Huff Post*, 23 January [Online]. Available at: www.huffingtonpost.co.uk/entry/ryan-gosling-oscar-nomination-ken_uk_65afd0d9e4b0f55c6e3107c8 (accessed 23 January 2024).

Kelly, A. (2023) 'This line in Barbie made a viewer issue a "warning" to other women', *She Knows*, 31 July [Online]. Available at: www.sheknows.com/entertainment/articles/2819538/barbie-movie-acceptance-speeches-scene-warning/ (accessed 1 August 2023).

Leese, T. and Barker, C. (2022) *Teach Like A Queen*. Abingdon: Routledge.

Mattel (2019) *The Dream Gap Project* [Online]. Available at https://shop.mattel.com/pages/barbie-dream-gap (accessed 1 August 2023).

Muir, R. (2022) '"Into the Unknown": Using facet methodology to explore the Disney Princess Phenomenon', *Methodological Innovations*, 15(2), 127–141 [Online]. Available at: https://doi.org/10.1177/20597991221090453 (accessed 1 August 2023).

Parker, K. T. (2017) *Strong is the New Pretty*. New York: Workman Publishing.

Sandberg, S. and Barksdale, L. (2023) 'Girls make great leaders. So why do we often tell them not to lead?', *USA Today Opinion* [Online]. Available at: https://eu.usatoday.com/story/opinion/voices/2023/07/27/sheryl-sandberg-lean-in-girls-women-leadership-inequality/70468645007/ (accessed 1 August 2023).

CASE STUDY 1

CONFRONTING UNCONSCIOUS BIAS

Rebecca Hoyes

Returning from maternity leave awakened me to unconscious bias. My colleagues often questioned me about why I returned to work full time, while my husband (who worked at the same school) was never questioned about how he would cope juggling work and a family.

The worst part was that it wasn't just male colleagues who appeared to have unconsciously biased viewpoints about my role as a working mother. Many female colleagues couldn't believe that I was back full time. This was the moment I knew I had to disrupt their thinking. Why couldn't I have a career and a family? Why couldn't I set an example to my children of a good work ethic? My parents were my role models and they both worked full time and were also teachers. I was determined to do something to change these outdated views.

Therefore, to confront the bias, I disrupted in the following ways:

- I noticed the bias. Realising that the bias exists is empowering. I deliberately hesitated to take on tasks others presumed I would do, such as ordering catering, taking minutes, photocopying for others. Next, I talked amongst female colleagues. I shared stories of where I had noticed unconscious bias being used towards pupils, colleagues, and me. The more awareness, the more people were noticing and sharing their experiences.
- I challenged biased behaviour. This is still an ongoing issue, but I felt exhilarated when I put forward an idea to male colleagues and was able to take credit for it. Admittedly, a few felt they had to explain to me why it was such a good idea, but nonetheless, I got the credit. In the past I have had my ideas introduced back to me as if they were original. I learned there was a term for this – 'hepeating' – and I now encourage others to be 10% Braver and point this out.
- I widened the circle. I enjoy being a social butterfly at work and I made an effort to widen my circle. I go to the staffroom, I chat to a variety of people, I sit with

colleagues at lunch. Sometimes, I even sit with the Head. Speaking to different people helps to better understand cultural and gender issues.

- I paused. In the world of teaching, we make hundreds of decisions daily. There is a danger that if we make decisions too quickly, they are made on assumptions, stereotypes, and bias. I have learned to pause. There are two sides to every story and somewhere in the middle is the truth. It is important not to believe the first thing you are told. Investigate and dig deeper if needed, but do not make assumptions and jump to the wrong conclusions.
- I do not make excuses. I am trying to give up making excuses to leave work before others and to not take the guilt home with me. I am working on that guilt, as who is judging me? And why should they? I know I do a good job and will be opening the laptop again once the children are in bed.

What bias do you experience and how will you disrupt this?

PART II

BREAKING BARRIERS

DIVERSE WOMEN IN EDUCATIONAL LEADERSHIP

INTRODUCTION

Natasha Hilton

In 2019 I attended my first Council of British International Schools (COBIS) conference and one of the workshops listed was being led by Vivienne Porritt. I attended and I felt like she was speaking to 'me'. Her passion for supporting and developing women to be confident seeped out of her – I wanted that confidence, I wanted to support others. The rest, as they say, is history. My journey into WomenEd started that day. That day I realised I was not alone. But I also realised I had a voice and I needed to use it to make change, to take action, to cause disruption!

The need for disruption is pressing. The dawn of a new era in education beckons, one that embraces varying perspectives, experiences, and voices that have long been silenced. The need for diversity in leadership has never been more apparent.

Women in educational leadership have often found themselves at a disadvantage, battling not only gender biases but also the additional layers of discrimination that come with being from diverse backgrounds. It's a perplexing paradox – the educational sector, traditionally seen as a bastion of enlightenment and progress, can sometimes be ensnared by its own biases. As the world evolves and the demand for dynamic, inclusive leadership surges, it is imperative that these barriers are dismantled.

The educational landscape poses unique challenges for women who identify as global majority, neurodivergent, LGBTQ+, or those with disabilities. For them, it is not just about breaking the proverbial glass ceiling, but about dismantling the entire structure of inequality within education, particularly for female leaders.

This section highlights these once silenced voices. It will navigate the intricate web of challenges that women from diverse backgrounds face. Women who have grappled with feelings of inadequacy when aspiring to leadership positions in education. However, the narrative doesn't stop at acknowledgement. The heart of this section is dedicated to showcasing the inspiring stories of women who have defied the odds, surmounted the barriers, and risen to leadership positions in education. These real-life accounts are beacons of hope, demonstrating that change is not only possible but inevitable. The narrative here isn't one of despair but of empowerment.

We will dissect each barrier with precision, examine the tools at our disposal, explore actionable strategies and initiatives that women can undertake to disrupt these barriers, not only for themselves but for the generations to come. Whether it's mentorship programs, allyship, advocacy, or institutional reforms, there are myriad ways women can drive change in educational leadership.

The women in this section have shattered barriers, made transformative changes. Together, we will embark on a journey to dismantle the barriers that have persisted for far too long, ensuring that future generations of women in educational leadership experience more equitable treatment and lead in more inclusive environments. (See: https://womened.com/diversity-campaign)

| حوا | Hawa|Eve|

define me not by the lunar bloodshed

my body is gifted with the

miracle of nurturing itself on cycle

i am mother and father

breadwinner and warrior

cramps and bleeding

lipstick and heels

are you not in awe

of the peace treaty i sell the world,

despite my growing pains?

i am beautifully woman | مبينا | MNH |

Mubina Husain

7

THE DIVERSITY GAP

WHAT IS THE CURRENT STATE OF PLAY IN EDUCATION?

Parm Plummer

KEY POINTS

This chapter will:

- show how schools seek to reflect their communities and student bodies and are beginning to diversify their staff body as a result
- explore how we define diversity as an important question to consider in challenging the status quo
- argue we need meaningful data to bring about clarity and understanding of the success of inclusive strategies.

Definitions

When exploring the question of diversity, it is easy to have conflicting views on what this means. For some, diversity is only about race or ethnicity. Certainly, when researching this chapter, it was easy to simply follow this narrow definition. However, this simplifies the issue of protected characteristics. WomenEd has always been clear that we wish to see more women from diverse backgrounds in leadership positions. For us, this means the intersection of race, for sure, and also sexuality, disability, age, neurodiversity and motherhood. According to Joslyn et al. (2018), diversity as a concept encompasses many qualities, some of which might be easily visible (for example, race, gender, religious affiliations and disabilities) and others less visible (for example, class or sexual orientation). Simply codifying diversity by people in the global majority belies the challenge that different networks in our global community face. For example, in Jersey, my locality, the challenge is to bring in more individuals from our hidden communities such as Portuguese and Polish women (and men too, as there is not enough visibility in schools of them either), as well as increasing ethnic representation. In international schools, the local community can be noticeable by their absence. Diversity must be about young people seeing themselves as this is what makes a difference to their progress and aspirations. For this reason, in this chapter, I will explore the breadth of views on diversity and define our aim as incorporating the characteristics outlined above.

What Does the Data Tell Us About Race in Education in the UK?

There are several sources to triangulate to establish a clear picture on how diverse education is. The main dataset for England is the school workforce census (Gov.UK, 2023) which gathers data in November each year. This tells us that in 2023:

> The ethnic diversity of the teacher workforce continues to increase, with 15.6% of teachers identifying as belonging to an ethnic minority group, up from 11.2% in 2010/11. Within these percentages, white minorities accounted for 5.3% of teachers.

> The proportion of teachers who identify as Asian or Asian British has increased by two percentage points since 2010/11, to 5.3% of the workforce. Over the same period, Black or Black British has increased by half a percentage point to 2.5% and Any Other Mixed Background by one percentage point to 1.7%.

This data suggests that things are improving, albeit incredibly slowly – 2% in 10 years?

When exploring teachers who were in leadership positions, in 2022/23, 15.5% were White British, 11.1% were White Minorities, 9.7% were of Black or Black British and 8.3% of Asian or Asian British.

This has changed over time. In 2010/11, 13.9% of White British, 8.0% of White Minorities, 8.1% of Black or Black British and 6.5% of Asian or Asian British teachers were in leadership positions.

According to this, when we consider race at leadership level, the picture is improving for minorities in all groups which have seen an approximately 2% increase over the past 12 years, albeit again glacially slow progress. However, the data gets more complex when we start to intersect data. The number of ethnic females in these leadership roles, and particularly at Headteacher level, is low, and in some cases there was not enough data for measurements to be meaningful. A minimal improvement is seen in some areas and some decreases in headcount over ten years, particularly in Asian and Black females. The report highlights:

> Middle leaders from Ethnic minority backgrounds were 14% less likely [to be promoted]. Senior leaders from Ethnic minority backgrounds were 15% less likely to be promoted to headship.

Similarly, Asian/Asian British and Black and Black/British were significantly less likely to be promoted (–23% and –15% respectively). The scale of the issue is seen in that 96% of Headteachers in 2021 were from a white ethnic background.

Interestingly, recent data has highlighted the disparity in employment of global majority teachers. London was an anomaly in terms of the numbers of ethnic teachers with 32% of teaching staff being of ethnic minority backgrounds in 2022. Of all English schools in 2016, 46% had no global majority teachers, with 16% of schools employing 20% of all Black, Asian and Minority Ethnic (BAME) teachers. At leadership level, 37% of leaders in London were from global majority (including White Minorities) backgrounds compared with the West Midlands (the nearest comparative location) having 14% of leaders. The North-East region has one of the least diverse teacher and pupil bodies in England, with 89% White British teachers and 86% White British pupils. The biggest ethnic minorities for pupils, other than mixed, are 1.5% Pakistani and 1.3% Black African origin with only 0.27% Pakistani teachers and 0.1% Black African teachers. Gorard et al. (2023) highlight that 'Most of these ethnic minority students will never encounter a teacher of similar ethnicity in the classroom'.

This concentration of non-white teachers in London highlights the lack of diverse representation across all schools, let alone at leadership level, and belies the progress that has been made.

If we turn now to the other UK nations, we see a similar story. In Wales, only 15 leaders identified as non-white and 7 of a total of 3,443 Headteachers were non-white ethnic, although none of these identified as of ethnic minority origins (Education Wales, 2020). In Scotland, we see a similar experience. The *Diversity in the teaching profession* annual data report identifies only 2.5% of ethnic minority teachers in promoted posts (Scottish Government, 2022). Finally, in Northern Ireland, the data was not available for any characteristic other than gender (Department for Education, 2023). In all cases, no published data was available for the intersection of gender and ethnicity, or disability or age.

When it comes to WomenEd's global community, the picture is even more difficult to ascertain. CIS carried out research in their member schools to ascertain a range of data, including ethnicity. Their report identified that 26% of leaders in schools were non-white and that a 'leadership team member is 3 times more likely to be white' (Neyra, 2021). In the United States of America, the most up-to-date figure for non-white teachers is around 18% (National Center for Education Statistics, 2019). In the United States, it was estimated that a student will be taught by about 55 individuals during their schooling, but that a Black student in Detroit (for example) might expect to have only one Black teacher during their schooling (Gorard et al., 2023).

Other than this data, there is a dearth of analysis of ethnicity at an international level.

The focus of this analysis so far has mainly been schools, but the pattern is reflected in higher education. The Equality Challenge Unit (ECU) published data which identified that there was a lack of representation at the top levels in higher education globally. According to this research, only 1.6% of professors and less than 1% of senior academic staff were global majority and female (ECU, 2016).

All of this suggests that as far as the data is concerned, there is a global lack of diverse representation at leadership level by race, and even more so when we combine race and gender.

However, it is fair to say that intersectional analysis is lacking in all jurisdictions. The limited data gathered on sexuality and disability highlights the challenging nature of data gathering. According to the Department for Education, less than 1% of the workforce had a disability, whilst 17.7% of the population has a disability (Belger, 2023). The School Workforce census does not contain data on disability due to the 'large amount of missing data' (Belger, 2023). This may suggest that schools don't value the importance of gathering this data, or that people are reluctant to disclose or acknowledge disabilities. A positive development is that the UK Department for Education included questions in the School and Colleges Panel Report (IFF Research, 2023), which explored insights into the reasons why teachers and leaders may not disclose their disability status to their school. Teachers and leaders were asked about any disability they might have, and whether they declared this to their school.

Findings from the June 2023 wave of the School and Colleges Panel were published in October 2023. Key findings are:

- One in five (19%) leaders and teachers identified as having a disability or a long-term health condition. Amongst school staff who considered themselves to have a disability, four in five (80%) had disclosed this information to their school or trust.
- Thirty-nine school leaders or teachers who had indicated they had a disability or long-term health condition had not disclosed it to their school or trust. The three most commonly selected reasons for not disclosing were:

  ○ A concern that they would be discriminated against
  ○ Concerns about how their personal data would be collected and stored
  ○ Their school or trust had not asked them to disclose the information.

This positive step in the UK enables schools to consider such data and take steps to use it to inform and improve policies and practices.

For sexuality, the issue becomes even more profound. Data gatherers are reluctant to request information on sexuality and it does not feature in the School Workforce census. This again could be the result of similar issues as identified for disability. In some parts of the world, openly acknowledging your sexuality could be dangerous. Thus, for both disability and sexuality, datasets are not yet reliable and do not provide a clear picture as to the full extent of diversity in our education. This ultimately means that we have very limited knowledge, other than anecdotal and lived experience accounts, of the numbers of women who identify as LGBTQ+ and those with disabilities in the school workforce, including leadership.

Employers must be bolder in trying to access this data, and anonymised surveys may help unlock this. It is hoped that acceptance of the need for verifiable and accurate data on all protected characteristics for the education workforce, and for leaders in particular, is necessary for the profession to ensure that it is representative and equitable and students can see themselves reflected in this workforce.

Disruptions

- System leaders/CEOs/Governments: Gather the data! You can only act on the problem if you can identify it. Without valid data that gives the full picture of what diversity looks like in your educational organisations (including all measures, such as sexuality, age, gender and disability) you will not be able to act to remedy the issue or monitor if policies you put in place are having an impact. Globally, compare the differences between organisations in different countries – are some better than others? Share good practice when you see it. Without such data gathering and analysis, any desire to effect change is ineffectual.
- Senior leadership teams: Consider what diverse looks like in your organisation. What does your student community look like and does your workforce and leadership and governance team reflect this? Consider developing a strategy to bring more of these communities into your organisation to make them visible.
- Middle leadership teams: Support future leaders to join networks or organisations such as WomenEd which will help them develop in their leadership journey. Such networks will amplify their voices and help them to be more visible and remembered when they apply for roles. You can also encourage them to take secondments or whole-school actions.
- Individuals: Lift and raise diverse leaders and be conscious of your own biases when recruiting or promoting. Many of these individuals will often only see themselves reflected in the cleaning, site management or catering staff in the school – be aware of this and educate yourself to acknowledge and use your privilege to bring about equitable change.

References

Belger, T. (2023) 'DfE told to fix disability data gaps for half of teachers', *Schools Week*, 23 February.

Department for Education (2023) *Education workforce* [Online]. Available at: https://www.education-ni.gov.uk/articles/education-workforce (accessed 30 June 2023).

ECU (Equality Challenge Unit) (2016) *ECU Equality in Higher Education Statistical Report 2016*. York: AdvanceHE.

Education Wales (2020) *Key facts: Ethic diversity in schools* [Online]. Available at: www.gov.wales/sites/default/files/publications/2020-12/ethnic-diversity-in-schools.pdf. (accessed 27 July 2023).

Gorard, S., Chen, W., Tan, Y., See, B. H., Gazmuri, C., Tereshchenko, A., Demie, F. and Siddiqui, N. (2023) 'The disproportionality of ethnic minority teachers in England: Trends, patterns, and problems', *Routledge Open Research*. Available at https://doi.org/10.12688/routledgeopenres.17798.2 (accessed 14 December 2023).

Gov.UK (2023) *School workforce in England* [Online]. Available at: https://explore-education-statistics.service.gov.uk/find-statistics/school-workforce-in-england (accessed 25 July 2023).

IFF Research (2023) *Schools and College Panel Report June 2023* [Online]. Available at: https://assets.publishing.service.gov.uk/media/6537e3e65e47a5000d989912/School_and_College_Panel_June_2023.pdf (accessed 28 April 2024).

Joslyn, E., Miller, P. and Callender, C. (2018) 'Leadership and diversity in education in England: Progress in the new millennium?', *Management in Education*, 32(4).

National Center for Education Statistics (2019) *Status and trends in the education of racial and ethnic groups* [Online]. Available at: https://nces.ed.gov/programs/raceindicators/spotlight_a.asp (accessed 1 July 2023).

Neyra, A. (2021) *What the data tells us about diversity in international school teaching staff and leadership* [Online]. Available at: www.cois.org/about-cis/news/post/~board/perspectives-blog/post/what-the-data-tells-us-about-diversity-in-international-school-teaching-staff-and-leadership (accessed 24 June 2023).

Scottish Government (2022) *Diversity in the teaching profession: Annual data report* [Online]. Available at: www.gov.scot/publications/diversity-teaching-profession-education-workforce-annual-data-report-2022/pages/5/ (accessed 20 July 2023).

8

TAKE YOUR SEAT AT THE TABLE!

Haley Yearwood

KEY POINTS

This chapter will ask:

- There is a lack of women from the global majority in school leadership, so how do you demonstrate that your seat at the table is not just a token gesture?
- As someone who does not fit the stereotypical leadership mould, how do you make your role distinctively your own and still feel comfortable?
- What can be done to support young global majority women at the start of their teaching career, enthusiastic and eager to make a difference?

Introduction

Being a senior leader can, at times, be a lonely endeavour. You are no longer part of the wider teaching body, but instead are part of a smaller, specialist group of colleagues. There are decisions that need a laser-sharp approach and these decisions are sometimes required to be made with little time for digestion or rumination. As a woman of colour, from humble beginnings, feeling like you 'belong' at the top can be difficult. The colleagues who you previously had an affinity with, due to culture or ethnicity, seem more distant. You have now stepped over the invisible line into whole-school leadership and the camaraderie seems less appropriate.

I distinctly remember a moment which epitomised my 'difference' a few years ago. I was a head of year at an outstanding school in inner-city London, and during one evening at the local pub (the usual end-of-term gathering) my colleagues started to share their GCSE results. I do not know how this conversation started, but there were about eight of us around the table and I was probably one of the few teachers there who had been educated in London and at a state school. As a teenager, my own comprehensive secondary school had a very poor reputation; there were regular fights, our GCSE results were amongst the lowest in the borough, and by the time I was in Year 11, a police van was resident at our gates every day at 3:30pm. Saying that, I enjoyed school and my results – six C-grades and three A-grades – were some of the best amongst my immediate peers. These grades had allowed me to study English literature and drama at A-level and then again at university. Low and behold, fast-forward 20 years and I was now on the leadership team, managing a year group. I felt I had achieved well and I had been the first member of my immigrant family to attend university. So you can imagine my trepidation as one by one my colleagues reeled off their GCSE results – there was a multitude of As and A*s. I was embarrassed. No one had mentioned anything lower than a B and I dreaded what they would think of me, on top of what I *already* perceived they thought of me.

Teaching at a school which has an ethnically diverse demographic is lovely and I saw parallels between my own childhood and those of my students. However, my fellow teachers were not from the same socio-economic backgrounds, and I was highly self-aware and paranoid, feeling that I was not as worthy of my role as they were. Their knowledge and wit seemed extensive and they exuded confidence. My undergraduate and Master's degrees seemed insignificant. I (perhaps) observed the raised eyebrows and the (mis)interpretations of students' behaviours. You see, what I saw as banter and jovial interactions between students were criticised and policed. Ethnic minority households are generally loud, whether it is the conversation of the household, or the music being played, or the visitors who 'pop in', and this translates to the playground when our children are communicating. When you understand the colloquialisms of the Black children and can code-switch in a way that other senior leaders cannot, you become conscious about how you, yourself and your community are perceived. Being from the global majority, students of a similar background enjoy and have an affinity with aspects of your identity that, in turn, you feel you need to downplay so that you are not too 'down with the kids'.

My seat at the table was well-deserved though. No one had just *let* me be a head of year for the sake of it. I had interviewed and made an impression and my year group was successful.

It is very important that you are kind to yourself. I relayed this GCSE incident to a friend, who wonderfully remarked that it was not a case of me having to feel privileged to be at a table full of other people who absolutely deserved to be there, but more of a case that I should be proud that I was holding my own amongst peers who, on paper, should be running the country. Comparison is a killer. You can worry that someone else has an advantage over you because of the university they went to, or the social class they come from, but ultimately your achievements are not diminished by anyone else's accomplishments. You are a trailblazer – because of your professional qualifications, experiences, and integrity. You have earned your seat, just as everyone else has. Often, the only one who needs your credibility proven is you. We can become so fixated on difference, so terrified of being 'othered', that we are blind to the common ground that we share with our colleagues which is one of success.

Being 'different' does not have to be a negative. With the realisation that you have earned your seat at the table should come the second realisation that your seat can be decorated however you please. A great method of taking stock and reflecting is simply by creating a 'Now, Next, Later' audit.

- What are you doing now professionally? What is happening in your educational setting that you are leading or implementing?
- What is next on the horizon? Short-term goals that are good to work towards and new ideas that are quick wins.
- What are you working towards in the long term? How will everything that you are doing come to fruition?

Barriers

Women's voices, particularly of those from diverse backgrounds, are needed more than ever to disrupt the status quo. According to the *Tes* magazine (Mason, 2022), female teachers are 'significantly less likely' to become Headteachers than their male counterparts, despite making up more of the workforce, with Department for Education data showing that 'men become headteachers earlier in their careers than women'. Global majority teachers (of any level) are much less likely to be led by a Headteacher or senior leaders who represent them culturally, or even by gender, as demonstrated in the chapter in this section by Parm Plummer.

When I was in Year 6, on the last day of school my Black female classroom teacher held a handful of us back at the end. She wished us the best of luck for Year 7 and our new adventure and ended her farewell with the words, '… you will have to work twice as hard to get half as far'. Her sentiment was lost on me and my 11-year-old naivety. It was only years later when I reflected on the women who had influenced me that I noted the caution in her last teaching moment with us. Her words also highlight the power of community, which is a tried and tested method for success for diverse women.

We must feel that we belong and are accepted, not simply tolerated. There is safety in numbers and those at the forefront of innovation and change in education must ensure that there is a profound support network for women: for Black, brown and Asian women; for women from challenging socio-economic backgrounds; for women at all levels of leadership. It is more than time to disrupt the status quo for these women.

Disruptions

- Imagine being a newly qualified teacher, bright-eyed and bushy-tailed, who is handed a directory of support networks and interest groups. A myriad of opportunities would open for those young women who no doubt throughout their career will question the validity of their seat at the table. These networks should be encouraged to promote both professional and personal innovation. We can explore a checklist of 'interests' when we sign up to a lifestyle app or website; we are able to curate our social media platforms; we can even choose what we digest on streaming apps – why not have the same as professionals in a challenging industry?

- These networks can be mandated by governments, for instance in the UK, starting on a borough level, with the model widened to national regions and even internationally. In a time of online meetings, webinars and podcasts, female teachers from the global majority would benefit from knowing where to reach for support from the outset of their career.
- It is important that, whilst networking is encouraged on a macro level, within schools themselves, new staff members should be made aware of any mentoring schemes which go beyond the usual Early Career Teacher (ECT) programmes. Where there may not be any, staff should be sign-posted to support groups.

I am now a Safeguarding Lead, in a different school, managing Mental Health and Well-being, as well as our PSHE curriculum and our Looked After cohort of students. At the start of my career, I would have loved to have met monthly with other Black and global majority teachers, to share and reflect with. In fact, I would absolutely love to have that now, 15 years in.

It can be lonely, but I know I am making a difference and whilst I definitely still have moments where I overthink an interaction or question how I may be perceived, I take stock and count my successes. You should too. Consider all that you have already achieved and all that you plan to do.

Pull your chair out and take your seat. You've got this.

Reference

Mason, C. (2022) 'Female teachers "significantly less likely" to become heads', *Tes*, 28 April [Online]. Available at www.tes.com/magazine/news/general/female-teachers-significantly-less-likely-become-heads (accessed 8 January 2023).

9

HOW DIVERSE IS IT 'REALLY'? THE DATA LINKED TO LEADERSHIP IN SCHOOLS

Miriam Hussain

KEY POINTS

This chapter will:

- show how diverse schools are in England
- explore the diverse leadership picture
- recommend next steps.

Introduction

My journey into teaching began in 2015, fresh out of university and ready for the world of work. I remember feeling privileged to make a difference, doe-eyed and naively, I might add. I have always worked in schools in inner-city areas with severe deprivation and a diverse student population. *I love this about my job*. I, myself, come from a dual-heritage background. At the time I didn't feel like my ethnicity stood out until I joined education. As innocent as it sounds, I didn't realise that the trainees that I had begun my career with were all white; the Senior Leaders and Trust Leadership of the school I joined were White British. I was oblivious but at the same time this had an unconscious impact on me. I didn't really have any career aspirations in education and had a Boxer-like mentality of 'must work harder' (Orwell, 1945). The turning point was on my first parents' evening: a parent had looked at the staffing board and asked me why the Senior Leaders were all white despite the pupils not being so. The school was 97% Non-White British and I didn't know what to say. It felt like someone had hit a switch in my mind. 'Why is senior leadership all white?'

The term inclusivity can be seen to be applied to any leadership team. Often a Headteacher will proudly declare their school leadership is representative of the community it serves. Students should be able to see themselves in school leadership roles most significantly in areas of extreme disadvantage. It doesn't only make me feel disheartened for the students, but also for educators from global majority backgrounds who aspire to be senior leaders. It makes it appear as a pipe dream rather than the next step. When it does happen, it appears as a Hunger Gameslike (Collins, 2008) task of how many qualifications are to be gained, roles to be executed and tasks to be done. If you happen to be a woman too, how you dress, how young and how assertively you come across are all factors. The list goes on. My first senior leader post felt like I had volunteered as 'tribute', being not only the youngest member of that team but also a minority due to my racial background. I was made to photocopy for the entire team during my first week so felt I was reduced to a stereotype.

This chapter is not saying that if you are a woman of colour you should get a promotion, but if you have the same skillset as your white counterpart you should be paid the same and have the same role. That moment with that parent is entrenched in my mind. Senior Leadership Teams should be representative of the communities they serve.

Context

A report on Racial Equality in the Teacher Workforce (2022) conducted by the National Foundation for Educational Research (NFER) found significant disproportions in teacher career progression. The research highlighted three components:

- substantial ethnic disparities in teacher career progression occur during the early career stages, particularly in Initial Teacher Training (ITT)
- at every step of leadership there are considerable ethnic disparities in progression
- women from the global majority are under-represented in Senior Leadership.

This report shows that not enough global majority individuals are successful in applying for Initial Teacher Training programmes and then succeeding in gaining a teaching role. They are then not supported to be developed to become senior or middle leaders. The research revealed that the lack of teachers from these backgrounds results in significant under-representation within Senior Leadership Teams (SLT). This narrows the diversity of the educational workforce as well as the cultural capital depth of those teams.

The NFER (2022) also found that Southern Asian practitioners were three times less likely to be promoted to senior leadership and Black practitioners were four times less likely to be middle leaders. In writing and researching for this chapter the key question for me is *why is this the case?* It is not wholly down to a low proportion of individuals from a global majority background applying, but also to a lack of opportunities within schools. Furthermore, Pearson conducted a report on diversity and inclusion in schools (2020) and found that one in three teaching staff felt that education did not reflect the diversity of students. This coupled with a lack of representation provides a damning picture.

The Data

The Department for Education (2023) released a school teacher workforce report and found that 92.5% of Headteachers are White British. Despite women making up 75.7% of the teaching workforce in every ethnic group, there are disproportionately more male senior leaders than women. Gendered stereotypes, bias, discrimination and imposter syndrome can be factors in whether women apply for the SLT roles. Additionally, women having children and going part-time significantly impacts these statistics. Delving into the data, only 0.5% of Pakistanis are Headteachers, 0.2% for Black African individuals and 0.1% for Bangladeshi origin.

Table 9.1 breaks down ethnicity and roles. White British made up 92.5% of Headteachers, 90.8% of Deputy Headteachers, 87.8% of Assistant Headteachers and 84.2% of classroom teachers. The White British cluster was the only group with the highest percentage consistently in the following leadership positions: Headteachers, Deputy or Assistant Headteachers and classroom teachers. What is prominent is how little each ethnicity other than white is represented in the figures. To put it in bleaker terms, *only* 7.5% of Headteachers in England are not White British.

Pearson's report on diversity and inclusion in schools (2020) across 2,000 teachers stated that 80% of teachers believe that more can be done to celebrate diverse cultures, whilst 66% felt that it was only until the Black Lives Matter movement that concerns for the inclusion of students and global majority individuals began to rise. Being a senior leader, working class and a woman of colour, the above statistics are shattering but not surprising. How does an individual compete with people who don't hold the above 'labels' and their starting point is much closer to the senior positions. *You just can't.* The playing field needs to be levelled with the barriers removed.

Teach First published an article regarding racism in the UK education system (2023) and found that global majority teachers face more barriers than White British teachers. This includes higher turnover due to moving schools or not remaining in the teaching profession. We need SLTs and governors to address this. Disruption is needed not only to get diverse people through the door to the teaching profession, but specifically on the progression of diversity into leadership roles and creating opportunities to do so. This is essential for systems and procedures to be amended or changed.

Table 9.1 Percentage and headcount of school teachers by ethnicity and role (Department for Education, 2023)

Ethnicity	All		Classroom Teacher		Assistant Head Teacher		Deputy Head Teacher		Head Teacher	
	%	Headcount	%	Headcount	%	Headcount	%	Headcount	%	Headcount
All	100.0	466.145	100.0	398.569	100.0	29.372	100.0	17.418	100.0	20.786
Bangladeshi	0.7	3.384	0.8	3.212	0.4	111	0.2	41	0.1	20
Indian	2.0	9.508	2.1	8.544	1.8	534	1.4	238	0.9	192
Pakistani	1.3	6.258	1.5	5.807	0.9	264	0.5	92	0.5	95
Asian Other	0.8	3.596	0.8	3.303	0.6	170	0.4	67	0.3	55
Black African	1.0	4.477	1.1	4.196	0.6	180	0.3	54	0.2	47
Black Caribbean	1.1	5.173	1.1	4.531	1.2	343	0.8	143	0.7	155
Black Other	0.4	1.719	0.4	1.583	0.3	77	0.2	29	0.1	29
Chinese	0.2	884	0.2	842	0.1	24	0.0	7	0.0	10
Mixed White And Asian	0.4	1.855	0.4	1.632	0.4	113	0.3	52	0.3	58
Mixed White And Black African	0.1	695	0.2	631	0.1	38	0.1	11	0.1	15
Mixed White And Black Caribbean	0.4	1.973	0.4	1.730	0.4	124	0.3	57	0.3	62
Mixed Other	0.6	2.768	0.6	2.511	0.5	134	0.4	65	0.3	58
White British	85.1	396.478	84.2	335.641	87.8	25.798	90.8	15.817	92.5	19.221
White Irish	1.4	6.659	1.4	5.510	1.6	476	1.8	316	1.7	358
White Other	3.8	17.820	4.1	16.234	2.9	855	2.1	365	1.8	367
Any Other Ethnic Group	0.6	2.897	0.7	2.663	0.4	129	0.4	62	0.2	43
Refused	N/A*	5.120	N/A*	4.544	N/A*	268	N/A*	126	N/A*	182
Unknown	N/A*	40.743	N/A*	36.057	N/A*	2.147	N/A*	1.121	N/A*	1.417

Implications

It is of paramount importance for organisations to tackle this gap to achieve an equitable system for education. Pearson's (2020) study on inclusive education discusses the mental toll due to race. They stated under-represented groups within education exacerbates loneliness and impacts on mental health. The charity Mind (2019) explores this further and stated individuals belonging to a minority group are more likely to experience anxiety. Environments where they are likely to be isolated will exacerbate this.

These reports raise the question as to how essential it is for all staff to feel included within a school environment. Pearson (2020) asked teaching staff to rate their overall health and happiness of their school community and found that those who felt under-represented within schools were not happy; 79% of teachers felt they were not reflected, which impacted on their mental health. The NEU (2020) found that pupils who have a real sense of belonging in schools were happier, more confident, and performed better academically.

The status of individuals of colour who have senior roles puts them on a pedestal because it's not the norm. These individuals become branded like 'superheroes' because they are rare. As Haddix (2017) states, 'it is not their responsibility alone to fix the problems with the education system'. From personal experience of being a senior leader, I had never experienced the number of questions about my age, relationship status, race and gender. I felt like I had to justify my roles with how many National Professional Qualifications I had achieved, how many degrees I had, but also how experienced I was, despite a very public gruelling interview process. School cultures need to normalise successful individuals of colour without the bombardment of invasive questions or prejudice.

Given the current data picture, it is imperative that we agree what can be done to empower women to apply for leadership positions. In England, the policy for improving the recruitment and retention of diverse teachers is unclear. Tereshchenko et al. (2020: 4) suggest the following guidance:

- The barriers for ethnic minority teachers are immense. Schools need to understand the scale and direction of these trends.
- Schools need to attract and nurture teachers to develop into leadership roles in the same vein as their white counterparts with regards to skillsets.

Tereshchenko et al. (2020) recommended SLTs make a conscious effort to improve the racial literacy within their teams. Racial literacy is a broad term; however, CEOs and SLTs do need training to close the gaps not only in ITT but also in SLT pathways. This can't be tackled by one administration but needs to be a collective and national approach. We all have a responsibility to champion and provide the right conditions within our educational settings. This starts at ITT recruitment and continues with the under-representation of global majority individuals within SLTs. Teach First (2023) have begun this work successfully as they are specifically supporting the racial diversity of applicants for ITT compared to previous years and other ITT programmes:

Our discrete choice experiment gave us a better sense of what we should focus on to attract more Black STEM students and graduates onto the Training Programme, but more research is needed to better understand whether/how the motivational profiles of different ethnic groups differ. (2023: 17)

This chapter highlights the urgent need for more diversity in SLTs. It is through consistently raising the profile of this data that the leadership picture will change. Individuals from all ethnic minority backgrounds need to be empowered and supported to be able to take on the responsibility and corridors of power. We must use our voices to be disruptive to do so.

Disruptions

What can we do to level the playing field for diverse women?

- Education organisations need to offer credible, high-quality mentors to guide individuals and support them into their next steps. Organisations like WomenEd, Litdrive, Teach First and Diverse Educators, to name a few, have a plethora of support to guide you to your next steps.
- Do your research for finding the right role. What are your non-negotiables with a school? Is your current workplace enabling you to flourish and preparing you for your next role? This will support you in finding surroundings where you can thrive.
- Learn from the lessons. Every negative experience provides a lesson. Toxic workplaces show the type of leader you'll never be, along with poor practices. Learning from the experience will ensure it won't happen again.
- Professionally network. Whether at a conference, a webinar or on social media there are educators able to support you outside of your school network to move to the next step.
- Build a profile. With the rise of social media, it has never been easier to blog, podcast, tweet, write articles and speak at conferences. Start small and allow this to support your career.
- If there is a deficit of development opportunities within your school, this gap can be closed by finding opportunities elsewhere. Reach out to an organisation or read articles. Whilst you are searching for the right role, supplement that time with the right research.

References

Collins, S. (2008) *The Hunger Games*. New York: Scholastic Press.

Department for Education (2023) *School workforce in England*. London: DfE. Available at: www.ethnicity-facts-figures.service.gov.uk/workforce-and-business/workforce-diversity/school-teacher-workforce/latest#by-ethnicity-and-type-of-school (accessed 19 March 2024).

Haddix, M. M. (2017) 'Diversifying teaching and teacher education: Beyond rhetoric and toward real change', *Journal of Literacy Research*, 49(1), 141–149.

Mind (2019) *Loneliness* [Online]. Available at: www.mind.org.uk/media-a/3124/loneliness-2019.pdf (accessed 2 February 2024).

National Education Union (NEU) (2020) *Creating a sense of place and belonging in schools* [Online]. Available at: https://neu.org.uk/advice/classroom/behaviour/creating-sense-place-and-belonging-schools (accessed 2 February 2024).

National Foundation for Educational Research (NFER) (2022) *Ethnic disparities in teacher progression occur during early career stages* [Online]. Available at: www.nfer.ac.uk/press-releases/new-study-shows-that-the-most-significant-ethnic-disparities-in-teacher-career-progression-occur-during-early-career-stages/ (accessed 2 February 2024).

Orwell, G. (1945) *Animal Farm*. London: Secker & Warburg.

Pearson (2020) *Diversity and inclusion report* [Online]. Available at: www.pearson.com/content/dam/one-dot-com/one-dot-com/uk/documents/educator/schools/issues/inclusion/diversity-and-inclusion-in-schools-report.pdf (accessed 2 February 2024).

Teach First (2023) 'Ethnic diversity and the teaching workforce', *Research Insights* [Online]. Available at: www.teachfirst.org.uk/sites/default/files/2023-04/2774%20Mission%2044%20research%20report%20v4_0.pdf (accessed 2 February 2024).

Tereshchenko, A., Mills, M. and Bradbury, A. (2020) *Making progress? Employment and retention of BAME teachers in England*. UCL Institute of Education: London. [Online]. Available at: at: https://discovery.ucl.ac.uk/id/eprint/10117331/1/IOE_Report_BAME_Teachers.pdf (accessed 2 February 2024).

10

LETTING GO OF IMPOSTER SYNDROME

WRITING HERSTORY

Loretta Fernando-Smith and Angeline Aow

KEY POINTS

This chapter will:

- show imposter syndrome has historically been defined as a feeling of self-doubt that is not connected to actual achievements or competence
- argue that the construct of imposter syndrome has the greatest systemic impact on marginalised groups
- help educators to question unconscious biases, self-talk and false narratives that uphold inequitable systems and perpetuate imposter syndrome
- call for action. Let's focus on fixing the systems and not ourselves.

Introduction

Have you ever been asked to present something to your colleagues, only to think: Who me?! Have you ever been nudged by a coworker to apply for a position, only to feel like you were not good enough? Have you ever stayed silent during a staff meeting because you felt like others had far more worthwhile things to say?

Then you have likely experienced imposter syndrome, a nagging feeling of self-doubt. The term imposter syndrome was first introduced in the 1970s by Pauline Rose Clance and Suzanne Imes. The professor and psychologist worked with highly success-ful female clients who had trouble internalising and accepting their achievements.

Despite their proven competency, capability, education, training and hard work, they often felt like frauds.

How It Manifests … the Data

Unfortunately, this feeling of not being good enough continues, to this day. Most women only apply for jobs when they meet 100% of the requirements. Even when they meet the criteria they are 16% less likely than men to apply for the job and 26% less likely to ask for a referral (Ignatova and Tockey, 2019). Women have been shown to have a 'professional confidence gap', and for LGBTQ+ and women of colour this feeling of being an imposter hits even harder (Nance-Nash, 2022).

Women are often told by well-meaning colleagues, friends and family to let go of this nagging feeling of self-doubt, to talk ourselves out of it: 'You've got imposter syndrome! Don't let imposter syndrome hold you back!' Perhaps we have even said these words ourselves to encourage a friend or to silence our inner voice. The problem with this stance is the assumption that we can talk ourselves out of it, that it is up to us to fix our mindsets; in effect, that the problem with imposter syndrome lies within us.

Learning Story – Loretta's WomenEd Deutschland Journey

One of my strongest experiences with imposter syndrome was when I was invited to join the WomenEd Frankfurt, Germany leadership team. At that point, I was an educator with over 15 years of experience working in multiple grade levels and multiple international schools. I had proven myself to be a competent, caring teacher and a thoughtful, supportive team-player. However, when I was asked to join the leadership team, I could not help shake the feeling that I did not belong. A leader? That was not me. I was a supporter, an enabler, someone who worked in the background and helped but I was not a leader. The term leader made me feel uncomfortable. I had learned to associate leadership with older, white, western and male – all the things I was not.

In 2018, 76% of American teachers were women, however, only 27% of superintendents were women. Sadly, this is a percentage that has remained consistent for the last 20 years and not just in America. This under-representation is even starker for women of colour: only 6% of principals in the US were Black women (Weiner, 2023). The bottom line is that there are too few women and too few women of colour in leadership.

So was it any wonder that I felt like I did not belong? Nowhere could I see myself in leadership.

Opposing narratives about motherhood, femininity and effective leadership styles served to further discourage me from wanting to associate myself with any references to 'leadership'. From a young age, girls are associated with 'sugar and spice and everything nice', perhaps the very opposite of assertive, strong, authoritative and commanding, the dispositions society often attributes to successful leadership. I was born in a former colony and emigrated to Canada at the age of 12. Through my upbringing, I later real-ised, I had unknowingly internalised attitudes of ethnic inferiority. I was a hardworking, friendly, petite, brown Asian woman, a mother, a wife. It felt irresponsible, rude and almost vulgar to want to be a leader. I could not be a leader while being all these things. The reality of my world built and validated my thoughts.

Learning Story – Angeline's Project Experience

I have been a pedagogical leader for more than 15 years, with a 20+ year career that includes:

- leading workshops at conferences and in schools across Europe, Africa, Middle East, Asia and the Pacific
- founding WomenEdDE (Germany) and four regional networks
- gaining additional qualifications including an MBA
- successfully fulfilling a variety of leadership roles in school.

However, I still struggled with arriving at a point where I valued my own worth and believed that I could successfully lead a project without collaborating with someone who had project experience.

I was approached by a senior academic to collaborate on a project which turned into a three-person endeavour. Throughout the project process, there were red flags and behaviours that epitomised toxic masculinity. I was naive and failed to acknowledge how I was being minimised as I wanted our project to be successful. As the behaviours continued, I reflected on the actions and the facts.

I realised that I saw myself as an educator leader through a white, male gaze and this had made me feel like a fraud even though I had envisioned the project's concept, suc-cessfully led training related to the project and contributed to its success as an experienced educational leader. Despite all that, ingrained in me was a belief that a person with a doctorate and who had worked in higher education was to be revered and it took repeated toxic behaviours for me to acknowledge that norms perpetuated by colonialism and patriarchal constructs made me devalue myself and falsely revere oth-ers. This resulted in me having feelings that are attributed to the label of imposter syndrome.

Essential Shifts

We have developed our sense of self-worth (or lack of) in societies that circulate values that have reigned supremely and dominated globally. As a result of colonisation our thinking as educators is underpinned by ideologies that are Western, capitalistic, patri-archal, hierarchical and more. These ideologies wield power in educational spaces and schools continue to reflect society's inequities where women do not have:

- equal rights
- equal access to resources
- equal representation in leadership
- equal recognition
- systems that are equitably responsive to their needs.

Therefore, the following shifts, as shown in Table 10.1, are essential if we are to be intersectional in our approach towards dismantling the systemic conditions that support gender inequity and imposter syndrome.

Table 10.1 How to dismantle systemic conditions that support imposter syndrome

Move away from ...	Increase emphasis on ...
feeling inferior as a result of cultural norms and unconscious biases	critical awareness of the role patriarchy and all systems of oppression play in perpetuating these feelings of inferiority
emotional reactions that lead to actions that solely focus on changing yourself	recognising that our emotions are a response to inequitable systems that require intentional actions to dismantle
fear of holding power in spaces	acknowledging that spaces where people have power and positionality are ones where there has been an under-representation of historically marginalised women
letting our self-talk and sense of self-worth deny us opportunities	seize opportunities by emboldening ourselves and others to leverage power, collaborate and co-design more equitable spaces
labelling internalised feelings of unworthiness as imposter syndrome	focusing on the facts, our achievements, and having a critical awareness of the systemic injustices and surrounding conditions that influence our perceptions

To make these essential shifts we need to tune into our own personal stories and be identity-conscious educators (Talusan, 2022). Knowing ourselves helps us be aware of our unconscious biases and internalised feelings of self-worth. It also helps us recognise how our reactions and feelings of being an imposter can be managed when we critically examine and deconstruct systemic injustices.

Loretta Shifting Her Story

Luckily I had women around me who nudged me to join the WomenEd Germany team. I stayed silent during the leadership meetings my first year, feeling like I had nothing to contribute. I volunteered to send out invitations, do the recordings or switch slides during gatherings in the hope that I could somehow contribute to the team. I talked to myself a lot that year: you have something to give, you are worthy of being here ... but somehow it didn't seem to help. I couldn't shake the feeling of being an imposter. Then I started to have a different conversation. I asked myself why – Why do you feel like you don't belong?

Why do you feel like you don't belong?

I started to see that the reality of my world was not the reality of life. I started to hear the sexist, colonial, biased stories that had sometimes intentionally been shouted and other times unsuspectingly whispered into my being. The problem wasn't me and my feelings of inferiority. The problem was an inequitable system that had no room for diversity and naturally created feelings of inferiority in members with marginalised identities. I had been gaslighted into thinking I was an imposter.

It was time to let go of imposter syndrome and instead acknowledge and actively work to change flawed systems. My shift in focus shifted my attitude. I decided to be what I could not yet see. I applied for leadership positions, I started to present and I started to write. With the encouragement of WomenEd I completed a Master's in Research. I did this by changing my belief that leadership was autocratic, all-knowing and dominating. WomenEd had shown me a different possibility: leadership that was collaborative, humble, caring, empowering and that lifted others up.

This leadership is not only possible but beneficial to an organisation as a whole. Research shows that women leaders inspire dedication and make the workplace more productive, collaborative and fair (Novotney, 2023).

Angeline Shifting Her Story

Hearing from my project sponsor that my expertise and leadership were more than enough was a turning point for me. It made me think of how Michelle Obama shared a secret about how she had been at every powerful table that one can think of and the realisation she had that the people around ' … are not that smart' (Da Silva, 2018).

It was a situation where I entered with hope, trust and a collaborative spirit only to leave feeling I had been exploited. I realised that there are many forms of incompetence that rise and succeed because of inequitable systems and structures. Patriarchal systems hold the WomenEd community back, create feelings of imposter syndrome for marginalised groups and are the same structures that promote incompetence for those possessing privileged identities (Chamorro-Premuzic, 2013).

I recognised that I didn't feel like I could be an author, a keynote speaker, a board member, a project manager or a founder because I had been socialised into thinking those positions were not for me. And if it did happen to me, I was lucky to be there because I had never seen a keynote speaker or international school Director who looked like me. After reading *Year of Yes: How to Dance It Out, Stand In the Sun and Be Your Own Person*, by Shonda Rhimes (2015), creator of *Grey's Anatomy* and *Bridgerton*, I now fully embrace her mantra:

I am not lucky. You know what I am? I am smart, I am talented, I take advantage of the opportunities that come my way and I work really, really hard. Don't call me lucky. Call me a badass.

Disruptions: Let's Write Herstory

What can we all do to counter inequitable systems?

- **Ask yourself:** What existing conditions, practices and systems have led to my belief of being an imposter? Which of my identities continue to perpetuate my belief of not being good enough?
- **Find community:** If you are not already a part of a WomenEd group, join one! Reach out to other educators via X (formerly Twitter) or LinkedIn.
- **Dismantle inequitable systems:** Stop gaslighting yourself and others. Stop spreading the myth that it is up to us to change our mindset. Recognise that there are systems in place that have made us feel inferior.
- **Watch Reshma Saujani (2023)** dismantle Imposter System and shift gendered stereotypes.

The world is full of stories. Some of these stories tell us that we are not leaders, they tell us what femininity is and that leadership and femininity do not mix, that motherhood and leadership are not compatible, that leadership looks, acts and feels a certain way. Some stories are just stories … they are simply not true! Whatever story is holding you back, step out of that story. Take charge of your story:

- Be what you want to see.
- Lift others up and collaborate.
- Success is an attitude.

You are not an imposter, the concept and system are the sham. You are smart. You are competent. You are capable. You are badass! Let's liberate our herstories from history. Start today!

References

Chamorro-Premuzic, T. (2013) 'Why do so many incompetent men become leaders?', *Harvard Business Review* [Online]. Available at: https://hbr.org/2013/08/why-do-so-many-incompetent-men (accessed 31 July 2023).

Da Silva, C. (2018) 'Michelle Obama tells a secret: "I have been at every powerful table you can think of … they are not that smart"', *Newsweek*, 4 December [Online]. Available at: www.newsweek.com/michelle-obama-tells-secret-i-have-been-every-powerful-table-you-can-think-1242695 (accessed 31 July 2023).

Ignatova, M. and Tockey, D. (2019) *Gender insights report* [Online]. Available at: https://business.linkedin.com/content/dam/me/business/en-us/talent-solutions-lodestone/body/pdf/Gender-Insights-Report.pdf (accessed 8 July 2023).

Nance-Nash, S. (2022) 'Why imposter syndrome hits women and women of colour harder', *BBC Worklife* [Online]. Available at: www.bbc.com/worklife/article/20200724-why-imposter-syndrome-hits-women-and-women-of-colour-harder (accessed 8 July 2023).

Novotney, A. (2023) 'Women leaders make work better. Here's the science behind how to promote them', *American Psychological Association*, 23 March [Online]. Available at: www.apa.org/topics/women-girls/female-leaders-make-work-better (accessed 8 July 2023).

Rhimes, S. (2015) *Year of Yes: How to Dance it out, Stand in the Sun and be Your Own Person*. New York: Simon & Schuster.

Saujani, R. (2023) 'Imposter syndrome is a scheme: Reshma Saujani's Smith College commencement address', *YouTube* [Online]. Available at: www.youtube.com/watch?v=BoHDDgeQtlc (accessed 2 January 2023).

Talusan, L. (2022) *The Identity-Conscious Educator: Building Habits and Skills for a More Inclusive School*. Bloomington, IN: Solution Tree Press.

Weiner, J. M. (2023) 'Fit to learn: March 2023', *NASSP* [Online]. Available at: www.nassp.org/publication/principal-leadership/volume-23-2022-2023/principal-leadership-march-2023/fit-to-learn-march-2023/ (accessed 8 July 2023).

11

A DIFFERENT KIND OF BRAIN

WHAT ARE THE BENEFITS AND BARRIERS OF NEURODIVERGENT WOMEN IN LEADERSHIP?

Yasmine Baker

KEY POINTS

This chapter will:

- explore what 'neurodivergent' really means, and how it can impact women in education
- share the experience of two different neurodivergent women in education
- discuss the limits imposed on neurodivergent women, both by themselves and the workplace
- highlight the ways that neurodivergence can enhance the personal qualities needed to lead in education.

Introduction

Attention Deficit Hyperactivity Disorder (ADHD) has long been mischaracterised as an excuse for naughty boys who can't sit still. I have heard countless colleagues criticise the overdiagnosis of ADHD to excuse the poor behaviour of primarily young, white boys who apparently cannot control themselves in a classroom because the symptoms of

ADHD are too easily associated with negative personality traits. Poor executive function becomes laziness. Emotional dysregulation becomes unchecked aggression. Inattentiveness becomes carelessness (Lebowitz, 2016). Growing up, I can recall at least three boys in my GCSE classes who were diagnosed with ADHD, and who were subsequently placed next to me so that I could be a positive influence on them.

I doubt that any of my teachers would suggest that me and my naughty desk mates displayed similar struggles in the classroom, let alone that we have the same neurotype. Teachers at parents' evenings would describe me as precocious and charismatic, a delight in the classroom. I was passionate about my academic success, consistently outperforming my peers.

But (and there was always a but) I could sometimes be too loud, too chatty, too clumsy. Not only that, but I was chronically late, often forgetful, and described as a girl with her head in the clouds which *could* have hindered my academic success.

It would take me over a decade to recognise that my struggles could be something more than just my own personal failings. After months of refusal from a doctor who was adamant that I was 'too intelligent' to be neurodivergent, I was referred to a psychiatrist and officially diagnosed with combined type ADHD.

In that same year I also completed my teacher training and was immediately promoted to Second in Department. Despite my success, I often felt like a fraud. The immense guilt I felt at having deceived the headteacher into paying me more despite my terrible habits led to a year of anxiety and overwhelm.

Following my diagnosis, I noticed that I was more sympathetic with myself. The things that made me, in my view, terrible at my job as a teacher made perfect sense, and I needed to reconsider my approach to school life. It was difficult navigating an education system designed for neurotypical people with a different kind of brain. I started to ask for the support I needed, and, in turn, encouraged others to be more open about their own needs.

This is not always how neurodivergent educators are treated, and it is even worse for women who are neurodivergent (Fenson, 2019).

This chapter aims to explore how women in education can embrace their neurodivergence and consider some of the ways that leaders in education can foster a supportive environment for neurodivergent women to develop.

What Does Neurodivergent Mean?

Neurodiversity is the idea that brain function is as unique as a fingerprint, no two brains work the same way. While most people are 'neurotypical' (i.e. their cognitive function results in typical patterns of behaviour), some people present atypical behaviours and thought processes, and would be considered neurodivergent.

The most known examples of neurodivergence include:

- ADHD
- Autism
- Dyscalculia

- Dyslexic
- Dyspraxia
- Tourette's Syndrome.

These neurological conditions impact the way that an individual interacts with the world, usually through communication, sensory input, emotional regulation, and information processing (Cambridge University Hospitals, 2023).

Judy Singer coined the phrase neurodiversity in 1998, sparking a shift in academic and cultural perceptions around these differences (Singer, 1998). Traditionally, these conditions would present major barriers to education and independence due to a lack of support, but Singer's model instead focuses on those strengths that can flourish when the correct accommodations are accessible to everyone. In education settings, Special Educational Needs and Disabilities (SEND) learners are at the centre of pedagogical discussion to empower educators to best support their progress and needs.

However, beyond school, access to accommodations and a positive approach to neurodivergence is inconsistent at best. From an education perspective, it is unclear how many neurodivergent women work within school leadership teams. And in general, openly neurodivergent teachers are few and far between. The Department for Education's latest census on professionals in education reported on a number of protected characteristics: disability was not one of them (Gov.UK, 2023).

So what is it about teaching and education that presents challenges to neurodivergent individuals?

Through a neurodivergent lens

My first case study will be my own experiences as a neurodivergent teacher whose diagnosis coincided with my promotion.

Following my diagnosis, it was clear why I found teaching overwhelming. Ultimately, my ADHD thrives under the structure of a school environment but I struggled with the constant deadlines that required data analysis, regular paperwork, and a solid organisation system. It seems ironic, then, that I would undertake training for a career that requires discipline, routines, and meticulous planning. While these are things that I struggle with, I know that my ADHD makes me a committed, creative, and empathetic educator. Luckily, I work in a supportive environment that encourages me to be open about my needs. Since my diagnosis the leaders in my school have given me the accommodations I need to not only survive but thrive.

My difficulty in even opening my books to start marking them was because reading 30 identical essays felt tedious and boring, so I would inject novelty to the task with the use of new technology purchased to enhance feedback. My poetry lessons were always well planned because I was passionate about the subject, so I developed poetry curriculum plans that helped inspire students and shared these with colleagues in exchange for their more exciting lessons on persuasive writing. I developed a routine so that I could work productively in the evenings and avoid taking work home, to protect my work–life balance.

Unfortunately, this is not the reality for many neurodivergent women in education (Wood and Happé, 2021). My second case study stems from conversations with a new colleague, Rachel.

Rachel was hired as Head of Geography in September, and we quickly became friends. She was sympathetic, honest, and willing to listen to my self-deprecating monologues before adamantly rejecting them. It didn't take long for me to disclose my diagnosis to her, to which she replied, '... that's ridiculous. I'm just like you but I don't have ADHD'.

Over the course of the next few months I would list off all of the ways my brain worked differently: the issues with organisation, the panicked rush to deadlines, and the overwhelm after a day of teaching loud students in a bright classroom. Rachel also struggled with these things, but instead of support and respect from her leadership team, Rachel's experience was shame, guilt, and believed it wasn't worth applying for a leadership role as she was unlikely to get it.

We worked together throughout the year to mitigate some of the issues we have during the everyday job. Together, we provide a safe space to commiserate over the barriers we face as neurodivergent women.

The Barriers

Teaching is a challenging profession, even without leadership responsibilities, and these can be compounded when coupled with neurodivergence.

There are three key issues that neurodivergent women can face in education:

- professionalism
- prejudice
- personal barriers.

These barriers are present in almost every facet of society, so it makes sense that they are prevalent in education. Not only do they make the job more challenging, but they can unfortunately result in a lack of representation of neurodivergent women, particularly in leadership roles.

Professionalism

Professionalism implies a level of competency and is considered a vital quality for any educator. However, it is a broad term that can be difficult to quantify. There are unspoken, universal rules that people are expected to inherently know and follow. ADHD and Autism, in particular, present challenges in understanding social norms, and these expectations are often broadly outlined in an employee handbook or are just understood to be the standard working expectation. For example:

- Rigid clothing and uniform expectations that don't accommodate sensory needs. Particularly for women, any unspoken expectation of makeup, high heels, and form-fitting clothing can be overwhelming.

- Expectations of communication styles and methods. Communication can often be indirect or couched in figurative language which can be challenging for neurodivergent people. Phone calls without visual cues from facial expressions can be difficult to understand, and some people may prefer email communication so that they can carefully draft their responses.
- Intense workloads and unmanageable working days. A long meeting scheduled after a full teaching day can present issues with focus or understanding. Sudden changes in plans and routines due to new initiatives being implemented midterm can cause anxiety. Of course, people should anticipate that extenuating circumstances can mean sudden change, but there should be support to help navigate these appropriately.

Prejudice

A lot of neurodivergent diagnoses rely on diagnostic criteria identified primarily in straight, white, cis boys, which unfortunately has caused a large percentage of the population to be misdiagnosed and mistreated (Young et al., 2018). As a result, many women seek a diagnosis later in life, often challenging medical professionals who mis-diagnose ADHD and Autism in women as anxiety or depression (Holthe and Langvik, 2017; Lebowitz, 2016).

For many women who are diagnosed later in life, feelings of guilt and shame are overtaken by anger and sadness for the lives they could have lived if they had had adequate support. Women see that their symptoms are not the same as their male coun-terparts, as often they are socially conditioned from a young age to mask their symptoms in day-to-day life in order to succeed (Lai and Baron-Cohen, 2015). Perhaps this is because of pervasive attitudes towards neurodivergence in society, or perhaps it is that there is not yet an established community to support women who are neurodivergent.

Personal barriers

Growing up neurodivergent can significantly impact how you see yourself. ADHD is often coupled with low self-esteem due to perceived rejection and hyper-awareness of the limitations of the disorder. Before the age of 12, children who have ADHD have heard 20,000 negative comments about themselves, and because ADHD can often cause emotional dysregulation and intrusive thoughts, these negative comments can stay with those children well into adulthood (Jellinek, 2010).

Rejection Sensitivity Dysphoria (RSD) is very challenging to manage and also rela-tively unknown. RSD is an overwhelming emotional response to perceived or real rejection, and disproportionately affects neurodivergent women. Women already face stigma for being emotional which is heightened with RSD (Young, 2017).

As an educator, emotional responses and interpersonal relationships are crucial for success. However, for many neurodivergent women, these are not easy to navigate. How can you face the perceived rejection of a child refusing to complete a task without getting overwhelmed? What do you do if you are sent an email with the wrong tone asking you to pop into your manager's office at the end of the day? While these may seem like minor professional communications, RSD can warp the perception of these incidents and make you feel small and rejected, thus causing a breakdown in your working relationships.

The Benefits

There is a shift in medical perspective to celebrate neurodivergent modes of thinking and qualities that are invaluable to enhancing education provision for everyone. Some of these qualities include:

- creative problem solving
- direct communication styles
- the ability to retain detailed factual knowledge
- pattern recognition
- hyperfocus.

While no two neurodivergent women are the same, all women deserve the opportunity to showcase their specific talents. When this happens, leadership teams and schools can truly benefit from a different perspective.

So how can leaders cultivate an environment that celebrates these qualities and supports women who are neurodivergent to overcome barriers?

From personal experience, there were two things that enabled my success: self-advocacy and open leadership.

Even before my diagnosis, there were particular aspects to my work style that most of my colleagues could tell you about. The fact that I stayed later than everybody else but never took work home, my insistence that conversations were followed up with emails, the assumption that I would take meeting minutes as I would never remember if it wasn't written down, and the countless hours volunteered to help with displays and resourcing are just some examples of the strategies I had found that helped me to succeed at work. It was not an overnight discovery; there was a lot of trial and (even more) error that resulted in missed deadlines and overwhelm. Over the years, my colleagues learnt how I worked best, and my managers could help me to organise the parts of the job that I struggled with.

When I was diagnosed, I really struggled with whether I should disclose or not. I was worried that I would be treated differently, that people would question my competency, and that I would be seen as a failure for asking for support. But I found the opposite to be true. My principal was incredibly supportive, and his first response was to offer me any accommodations I needed. My immediate line manager had been aware of my journey to diagnosis but she didn't need to change the way she worked with me, because the accommodations were built into our relationship. Even the vice principal who oversaw our department offered support, stepping in to look after my class when I had an emergency appointment. All my appointments were honoured, and there was never any question of my competency.

The things that made this possible were my openness as well as the relationships with leaders that had been fostered in the school. While I was still hesitant to share, I knew that it was better to be honest about my needs.

The accommodations I asked for were not huge, but they alleviated a lot of pressure so that I could be successful. Accommodations are personal for everyone, but can include:

- flexible start/finish times
- sharing information before meetings
- brain breaks/fidget toys allowed during meetings
- specific and preferred communication methods
- support communicating with parents in person or on the phone
- allowing the use of sensory aids (noise-cancelling headphones, ear plugs, fidgets)
- designated work areas with specific independent work time to minimise distractions
- asking a colleague to set smaller, manageable deadlines and hold you accountable.

The most important thing to remember is that neurodivergence does not have to be a barrier to success. In fact, it can be one of the things that makes you a successful and compassionate leader.

Earlier this year, Rachel and I had the opportunity to prove this to be true. We delivered a presentation to the entire staff body on how the brain works, why certain students display certain behaviours, and how to navigate emotional dysregulation as an educator to help support your students to thrive. This was well received across the school, and the strategies we discussed have been used by many staff members throughout the year. The session was quite personal, and although we have not disclosed our neurodivergence to the entire staff body, our openness about our difficulties and perspectives encouraged others to share their challenges. Colleagues even now share the impact of our training, and that would not have been possible without a supportive leadership structure that encouraged neurodivergent thinking.

For most of my life I have only seen the negative in how my brain works, my neurodivergence manifesting as inherent, immovable, impractical traits that I needed to mask in order to be accepted. Since my step up into leadership, and since accepting that I have a different mode of working, I have found that my neurodivergence is one of my significant strengths as a leader.

As educators, we work to support students with SEND, yet when students leave school, they are too often left to accommodate themselves, adapting to fit the neurotypical world. This must change. Leaders must also cultivate an open and safe working environment for their neurodivergent staff. I was allowed the accommodations and support that I needed to thrive, and, while I may not always be on time, the distinct positives that I bring far outweigh any negatives.

Disruptions

For the cultural shift necessary for neurodivergent women to succeed in leadership, there are three things that need to happen:

- People need to feel supported and appreciated for their neurodivergence.
- More research must be conducted on neurodivergent teachers and leaders and their experience at work.
- Neurodivergent women need to acknowledge their own strengths and believe in the positive impact they can have on a wider school community.

References

Cambridge University Hospitals (2023) *What is neurodiversity?* [Online]. Available at: www.cuh.nhs.uk/our-people/neurodiversity-at-cuh/what-is-neurodiversity/ (accessed 14 December 2022).

Fenson, Z. (2019) 'The female burden of neurodiversity', *The Week*, 10 December [Online]. Available at: https://theweek.com/articles/878719/female-burden-neurodiversity (accessed 14 December 2022).

Gov.UK (2023) 'School workforce in England' June [Online]. Available at: https://explore-education-statistics.service.gov.uk/find-statistics/school-workforce-in-england (accessed 28 April 2024).

Holthe, M. E. G. and Langvik, E. (2017) 'The strives, struggles, and successes of women diagnosed with ADHD as adults', *SAGE Open*, 7(1).

Jellinek, M. S. (2010) 'Don't let ADHD crush children's self-esteem', *Clinical Psychiatry News*, 1 May [Online]. Available at: https://cdn.mdedge.com/files/s3fs-public/issues/articles/70231_main_7.pdf. (accessed 14 December 2022).

Lai, M. C. and Baron-Cohen, S. (2015) 'Identifying the lost generation of adults with autism spectrum conditions', *Lancet Psychiatry*, 2(11), 1013–1027.

Lebowitz, M. S. (2016) 'Stigmatization of ADHD: A developmental review', *Journal of Attention Disorders*, 20(3), 199–205.

Singer, J. (1998) Odd People In: The Birth of Community Amongst People on the Autism Spectrum: A Personal Exploration of a New Social Movement Based on Neurological Diversity. Honours Thesis presented to the Faculty of Humanities and Social Science, the University of Technology, Sydney.

Wood, R. and Happé, F. (2021) 'What are the views and experiences of autistic teachers? Findings from an online survey in the UK', *Disability & Society*, 38(1), 47–72.

Young, E. (2017) *Do women really show their emotions more than men?* [Online]. Available at: www.bps.org.uk/research-digest/do-women-really-show-their-emotions-more-men (accessed 14 December 2022).

Young, H., Oreve, M. J. and Speranza, M. (2018) 'Clinical characteristics and problems diagnosing autism spectrum disorder in girls', *Archives de Pédiatrie*, 25(6), 399–403.

12

DIVERSE LEADERSHIP

IF YOU CAN'T SEE IT, BE IT!

Azuraye Williams

KEY POINTS

This chapter explores:

- my personal journey to develop as a diverse leader
- how a like-minded community can empower you.

Introduction

Over the past few years, there have been many organisations that have spoken out about the need for diverse leadership. Data, knowledge and experiences show that as well as a low number of leaders from a global majority background, there is also an even lower number of women of colour who lead education. A few years ago, I was someone looking up at leadership and thinking, why does no one look like me? These thoughts brought together a multitude of emotions:

- Am I good enough?
- Maybe this is my limit?
- If no one else has done it, what makes me special?

These emotions add to the bigger picture and statistical data that consumes us every day. After being a teacher for ten years who had expressed desires to move into leadership, I became a senior leader in 2021. In the previous year, I became a Diversity, Equity,

Inclusion and Belonging Lead for my Multi-Academy Trust of 21 schools. This chapter will explore the personal and professional developments that influenced my journey. It will also share my dedication and perseverance which supported me to develop into an inclusive leader with my own ethos, drive and moral purpose. This is something that many diverse teachers face when navigating their way into senior leadership as it can come with its own challenges.

The Early Stages

As a Black child growing up in our education system, I did not see anyone in leadership that looked like me and when I entered the teaching profession, the leadership structure presented the same stereotypical experiences that I had seen from school. As a young early career teacher (ECT), I was very optimistic about my career and the opportunities that lay ahead for me. I was quickly offered multiple learning and development opportunities that, at the time, felt very progressive but later felt like a stalling tactic. It can be very hard to understand how to progress when you are not able to see progression. I struggled after a few years as there did not seem to be any opportunities for me. I would see many people come into my school as ECTs and see them progress quickly in their career, while mine seemed to stand still. In recent years, I have really understood the importance of belonging within a workplace and my early experiences created an atmosphere that made me feel like I did not belong. My story is not uncommon, but how can we fix this?

Change

It is time to make a change to the diversity within education leadership. WomenEd is a driving force for this through their work around promoting and empowering women leaders in a predominantly male-led secondary environment. They are also inspiring more diverse leaders. One way to ensure equitable change is to support women leaders in their own diverse leadership. Organisations need to ensure that they are providing pathways for women leaders and supporting them through their journey.

Creating and Crafting Your Role

In 2020, in the midst of a global pandemic, education was forced to take a new direction. At the time, I was a Year 6 teacher aspiring to be a senior leader. During this time, the world witnessed the murder of George Floyd. This affected me personally and I felt that something had to be done. I contacted the CEO of my Trust and arranged a meeting with her to discuss how we could develop representation and diversity within our organisation. This was also an area of the education system about which I felt passionate.

After the meeting, my CEO was extremely supportive, positive and enthusiastic about pursuing greater diversity and belonging across our Trust schools. She was also very clear that she wanted this to be authentic and not tokenistic. This is also something that I agreed with, and we discussed how we could inform the senior leaders within the Trust about our plans.

Within my Trust there were very few leaders from a global majority background and this was also an area that I wanted to improve in our Trust. I used this opportunity to share a presentation with trustees, Headteachers, senior leaders and Trust-wide curriculum leads. I wanted to ensure that there was a shared message that was evolving throughout our Trust. At the time I did not realise that, through creating this opportunity for myself, I was naturally showing and developing my leadership skills, my communication skills, and the skills to share my vision and goals to develop alignment with a team. It is important that as a leader you can show these skills and motivate your team to be committed to your goals and values (Coalter, 2018: 30). I was unaware at the time, but this eventually led to me becoming our Trust's Diversity, Equity, Inclusion and Belonging Lead. This opportunity that I had created for myself came from my own personal drive and passion for something that I believed needed to be done. Did I have self-doubt? Yes! Did I feel that I was not experienced enough for this? Yes! Did I let this stop me? No! Daniel Pink (2018: 8) discusses the importance of intrinsic motivation, and due to the nature of this role, I was extremely motivated and passionate.

One of the main strategies of change is to focus on the human resources processes and procedures. As a Diversity, Equity, Inclusion and Belonging Lead, I find this to be one of the most important elements to support progression for diverse leaders. Alongside this, there should be open, honest and 10% braver conversations within your organisation. Policies can be created but cultures need to be challenged. This is an area that I have ensured has been central in my role. I have had honest and open conversations with Headteachers and senior leaders which has made them think about their leadership in relation to diversity and inclusion. It is important that senior leaders are present in these conversations as they help to drive the change. Initially I was creating these spaces to have these conversations without a school leadership title. This is often the case in many schools, but there must be someone who is willing to start these conversations, and more often it is not the senior leadership team. You can be 10% braver to ensure you are driving this change in your own school community.

Being a part of the WomenEd community has provided me with the skills and empowerment to challenge normal practices. As a diverse leader, it is important that our voices are heard, as well as having a seat at the table.

Developing Your Own Supportive Community

During the time that the world was going through the pandemic, I found this very challenging. This ignited my drive to become a senior leader, and social media (in particular X, formerly Twitter) was an outlet for me. I asked the Twitter community if there was anyone who would be willing to coach or mentor me through my own leadership journey and development. This tweet opened a new world to me. A few fellow Black women who were senior leaders reached out to me and I was able to connect with them. From this, my own support network and social circle of fellow Black women educators grew in a safe space where we met, had discussions and uplifted one another when we were celebrating our success, but also when we had workplace difficulties.

This was extremely inspiring for me as I had not been surrounded by any diverse leaders, and the words that always resonated with me are from Marian Wright Edelman (n.d.) who said, 'You can't be what you can't see'. I did not have role models to allow me to see myself as a leader. Owen Eastwood (2021) highlights the importance of belonging. A sense of togetherness and belonging is an inner need that we all share. Within my previous role, I did not have a sense of belonging to my own culture and how this was incorporated to my educational career. The community of ethnic educators that I met online opened a new world to me. I also connected with different companies such as Diverse Ed and I started to invest in my own senior leadership role by completing a course with Aspiring Heads. This course became another one of my safe spaces.

Community

Being a part of the many communities that I have spoken about in this section has supported me to drive change, challenge situations and empower myself. A real sense of belonging is important to ground you, as well as inspire you. Becoming a diverse leader will present challenges and surrounding yourself with a community of people who can support you is something that I encourage. It is important to create your own open and safe spaces. Coaching and mentoring is another avenue that many diverse leaders use. Many have found that finding a mentor or coach who can relate to their personal situations can prove to be extremely helpful.

Driving Change

In 2021 I gained an Assistant Headteacher post. When I received the role, I initially was struck with imposter syndrome. When you look at leadership, you expect all leaders to always have the answers. Being new to leadership, I wanted to ensure who I was an authentic leader and my natural personality is to be inclusive and drive a future of belonging. This was hard for me initially as I did not see any other leaders who looked like me and I was also the only Black teacher in my whole school. This made me look at my previous motto, 'You can't be what you can't see' (Edelman, n.d.). I wanted to make this more inspiring for other leaders like me so I started to think 'If you can't see it, be it'.

I had joined a very inclusive school community with a forward-thinking vision. This is not always the situation that diverse leaders experience, which is why it is important to research the school's ethos and values to ensure they align with your own. The school welcomed my inclusive ideas and strategies to support Diversity, Inclusion and

Belonging across our whole-school community. Even with this environment, it is still easy to feel the pressures that come with being a diverse leader.

Through my role as the Diversity, Equity, Inclusion and Belonging Lead for my Trust, I was able to support schools to look at their curriculum and their school ethos to ensure that they were also providing an inclusive environment. As a leader who wants to drive change, it is important that you develop your own confidence and look for opportunities to be 10% braver. The WomenEd community supports all women to seek these opportunities and I was able to use this to craft my own leadership journey and hopefully inspire others to create their own pathways.

Disruptions

It is important that we focus on global changes and the effect that these can have to disrupt the current challenges that diverse women face in order to develop and thrive in leadership roles.

- Organisations need to look within their workforces and current policies to see the challenges that diverse women face and develop strategies to support them. Many of these challenges need to be tackled within the recruitment phase.
- Organisations should think about the opportunities that they are presenting to women and ensure they are provided with equitable opportunities to develop and progress within their roles.
- On-going training is required in relation to Diversity, Equity, Inclusion and Belonging and the important factor is that this training needs to be ongoing.

Finally, change cannot happen if the working environment is not challenged! Choose to Challenge.

References

Coalter, M. (2018) *Talent Architects: How to Make Your School a Great Place to Work.* Woodbridge: John Catt.

Eastwood, O. (2021) *Belonging: Unlock Your Potential with the Ancient Code of Togetherness.* London: Quercus.

Edelman, M. (n.d.) *30 best Marian Wright Edelman quotes with image* [Online]. Available at: www.bookey.app/quote-author/marian-wright-edelman (accessed 15 December 2023).

Pink, D. (2018) *Drive: The Surprising Truth About What Motivates Us.* Edinburgh: Canongate Books.

13

HOW DO WE LEVEL THE PLAYING FIELD?

Radha Badhan

KEY POINTS

This chapter will:

- highlight that increasing levels of global majority educators are leaving education
- explore the persistent barriers that prevent the progression of global majority educators into senior leadership roles
- argue that there is a lack of genuine commitment to aid career progression for global majority educators.

Introduction

Being told that I had *only* made it into my role as an educator because I was 'cherry-picked as a woman, which ticked a second box' was tough to hear, knowing that the first box being referred to was my race. In this moment, the years of hard work, dedication and sacrifice meant nothing, and I felt like a complete imposter. Desperate for guidance and support, I turned to my leaders only to be told to 'toughen up' and that there had been a clear 'misunderstanding', which were even harder comments to digest. It was in these moments that I made the decision to leave my dream career of teaching. Unknown at the time, it was also in these moments that I was silently blossoming, finding my voice, and crafting my own journey to growth, healing and leadership.

As global majority educators navigate their way through potholes, mudslides and uneven terrain, their journeys to leadership are tougher with increased obstacles and barriers than their white counterparts (Lock and Worth, 2022). The School Workforce data for the UK for 2021/22 from the DfE (2023) only serve to confirm such hardship and highlight that so few global majority educators make it to the role of headship within the UK:

- 92.5% of UK Headteachers were white
- 4% of UK Headteachers were from the global majority
- 3.5% of all female Headteachers were from the global majority.

Whilst these figures sit in a wider context and discussion over global majority representation within educational leadership, they also serve to highlight the clear disparity in the playing field. Global majority women are simply nowhere near achieving equity in opportunity to access senior roles. So, how then can one talk about levelling out the playing field for global majority women in educational leadership when the field remains uneven for global majority educators as a group?

As someone who identifies as an Asian, female, UK Headteacher, this figure is somewhat alarming, isolating and leaves one feeling despondent. Therefore, my aims are to replace feelings of disillusionment with hope. This chapter will draw upon a mixed method approach and use both qualitative and quantitative data from five UK global majority Headteachers and their common enablers that empowered them to access and even dare to play on this uneven playing field.

Most importantly, I hope this chapter will serve as a beacon to light the pathway to help and inspire you on your own educational leadership journey.

Potholes and Mudslides Matter

The UK is becoming more diverse and multicultural; global majority students make up 35.7% in primary and secondary schools, yet only 4% of UK Headteachers are from the global majority (DfE, 2023). But why does this huge discrepancy between the representation of leaders to pupils matter?

Having global majority educators in senior roles challenges ideals of white superiority and discrimination (Ashe et al., 2019). Children who see people who look like themselves in positions of power develop a sense of ambition, relatedness, motivation, aspiration and belief that they too can achieve their own goals (Bunce et al., 2019). Furthermore, full representation at the most senior level creates inclusive environments where people from the global majority feel valued, respected, and genuinely part of their communities which leads to increased productivity and outcomes (Fischhoff, 2021).

Uneven Terrain Means Uneven Footing

Whilst it is acknowledged that teacher retention is an issue in the UK irrespective of race, 'applicants recorded as Black have the lowest acceptance rate' for Teacher Training courses (Gorard et al., 2023) and more global majority educators leave the profession than their white counterparts (DfE, 2023). This can be owing to the fact that from the onset in setting out to be a teacher, these educators are not on an even playing field.

Global majority trainees experience higher levels of anxiety from racist encounters during their initial teacher training (Wilkins and Lall, 2011). Once passing this first year, they are more likely to struggle to secure a permanent role and start their careers as supply teachers due to the discrimination they face during recruitment (Haque and Elliott, 2018). Once employed, they often start on lower salaries compared to their white counterparts (Janes, 2022) and continue to face racism in the workplace.

Alongside this, key reasons for their departure are their hidden workload, biases and micro-aggressive behaviour experienced in the workplace, leading to burnout and poor mental health (Pizarro and Kohli, 2020).

Stuck in the Mud

Overcoming such obstacles, some global majority educators are promoted to middle leadership and stay in such roles (Tereshchenko et al., 2020). Wallace (2020) suggests that this is because schools want to give the false impression of addressing diversity, whereas the reality is the preservation of white privilege continues to dominate senior roles.

Furthermore, the structural barriers and lack of representation amongst the highest level of governance, creates stagnation. Only 5% of governors and trustees are from global majority backgrounds (Weale, 2021), leaving them unrepresented at these top levels, hindering their progression and the ability to influence greater diversity in recruitment.

Additionally, the lack of and rejection of professional development opportunities has denied the progression of global majority educators (Clare et al., 2016). They are also more likely to be overlooked for promotions, providing a firmer barrier (Haque and Elliot, 2018).

Lastly, their increased susceptibility to imposter syndrome, due to the additional external challenges they have encountered (Levchak, 2018), has a long-term personal impact and can pose a barrier to their progression.

Whilst this picture seems a self-fulfilling prophecy, and a struggle to overcome these barriers, there is a way forward.

Equalising and Levelling Up

How can we change the narrative? And how can we start to equalise this playing field? After interviewing five UK global majority senior leaders, some commonalities became clear in how they progressed into leadership roles.

Firstly, all participants identified a key individual who had helped open the door of opportunity for them. Miller (2016) refers to this as white sanction, where white people act as gatekeepers. Global majority people face greater challenges accessing white dominated spaces so white people openly endorsing and enabling them is paramount to their success and progression.

Furthermore, mentoring proved vital for their career progression, having a positive impact on their self-confidence and self-belief. Whilst Elliot's work (2021) appreciates that imposter syndrome is irrespective of race, my participants voiced feelings of isolation, inadequacy and incapability. Mentoring allowed them to express their truth in their own way (Oberholzer, 2019), shake off their imposter, and feel less isolated in navigating their leadership journeys.

Undertaking relevant qualifications was key to my participants' progression (Choudry, 2019). Despite comments suggesting that my participants felt that undertaking qualifications was a tick-box exercise, the analysis demonstrated that those who had specific leadership qualifications had, in the end, secured leadership roles.

My participants expressed having to adapt and adjust part of their authentic selves to secure leadership roles. Often, global majority educators have progressed further when they look like and share cultural habits and behaviours similar to white teachers (Miller, 2015). Arguably anyone, regardless of ethnicity, moving into educational leadership may change, transition and adopt a different identity (Kelly, 2018). However, having to leave one's identity at the door leaves many global majority educators feeling uncomfortable. Nevertheless, Browne (2020) argues that when individuals address this false sense of self, they will be able to take the path of ethical leadership whilst maintaining a true sense of themself. Thus, the solution may be to find a middle ground and consider what is important to your identity.

Lastly, my participants expressed that both professional and informal networking were key to their progression (Callender, 2020). Having a sense of belonging, camaraderie and understanding encouraged them to feel empowered and supported on their paths to leadership.

Disruptions

How to level the playing field as an individual:

- identify a gatekeeper
- find a mentor
- leave your imposter at the door
- undertake Professional Learning and Development
- network, network, network: the WomenEd community is essential and our unconferences are a great support (WomenEd, 2021).

How to help level the playing field within your community:

- challenge institutions and their culture
- endorse and enable global majority individuals

- educate and promote the importance of global majority representation through to the highest ranks of your organisation
- genuinely commit to changing the narrative.

I hope this has brought some comfort to those feeling isolated or feel they have hit their concrete ceilings (Choudry, 2019). I implore you to smash through it. You are not alone and from every story of hardship and heartache can come hope, healing and headway.

This path is by no means an easy feat, and there will be moments of solitude, sadness and soul searching; however, I am certain that you will find your place.

References

Ashe, S., Borkowska, M. and Nazroo, J. (2019) *Racism Ruins Lives: An Analysis of the 2016–2017 Trade Union Congress Racism at Work Survey*. Manchester: Trade Union Congress.

Browne, A. (2020) *Lighting the Way: The Case for Ethical Leadership in School*. London: Bloomsbury.

Bunce, L., King, N., Saran, S. and Tablib, N. (2019) 'Experiences of black and minority ethnic (BME) students in higher education: Applying self-determination theory to understand the BME attainment gap', *Studies in Higher Education*, 1, 1–14.

Callender, C. (2020) 'Black male teachers, white education spaces: Troubling school practices of othering and surveillance', *British Educational Research Journal* [Online]. Available at: https://bera-journals.onlinelibrary.wiley.com/doi/10.1002/berj.3614 (accessed 15 December 2023).

Choudry, S. (2019) 'Concrete ceilings and kinked hosepipes: Understanding the experiences of BME female leaders in schools', in V. Porritt and K. Featherstone (eds), *10% Braver: Inspiring Women to Lead Education*. London: SAGE Publications Ltd.

Department for Education (2023) *School workforce in England, Reporting year 2022* [Online]. Available at: https://explore-education-statistics.service.gov.uk/find-statistics/school-workforce-in-england (accessed 15 December 2023).

Elliot, J. (2021) 'Imposter syndrome: "I didn't think I looked like a headteacher"', *Independent School Management Plus* [Online]. Available at: www.schoolmanagementplus.com/heads-governors-school-leadership-governance/imposter-syndrome-for-a-long-time-i-didnt-think-i-looked-like-a-headteacher/ (accessed 15 December 2023).

Fischhoff, M. (2021) 'How diversity increases productivity', *Network for Business Sustainability*, 19 January [Online]. Available at: https://nbs.net/how-diversity-increases-productivity/ (accessed 14 December 2023).

Gorard, S., Chen, W., Tan, Y., See, B. H., Gazmuri, C., Tereshchenko, A., Demie, F. and Siddiqui, N. (2023) 'The disproportionality of ethnic minority teachers in England: Trends, patterns, and problems', *Routledge Open Research*. Available at https://doi.org/10.12688/routledgeopenres.17798.2 (accessed 14 December 2023).

Haque, Z. and Elliott, S. (2018) 'Visible and invisible barriers: The impact of racism on BME teachers', *The Runnymede Trust and NUT*, 3 September [Online]. Available at: https://neu.org.uk/media/2936/view (accessed 20 March 2024).

Janes, W. (2022) 'Teachers' union calls on Government to address ethnicity pay gap', *Independent*, 8 January [Online]. Available at: www.independent.co.uk/news/uk/naht-asian-government-teachers-gender-pay-gap-b1989093.html (accessed 14 December 2023).

Kelly, B. K. (2018) Investigating Applicants' Perceptions of the Recruitment and Selection Process of Headteachers in English Secondary Schools: Looking at Headship Through a Leadership Identity Lens. EdD thesis, The Open University.

Levchak, C. (2018) *Microaggressions and Modern Racism: Endurance and Evolution*. Cham: Palgrave Macmillan.

Lock, H. and Worth, D. (2022) 'Why teaching still has a diversity problem', *Tes*, 20 April [Online]. Available at: www.tes.com/magazine/analysis/general/why-teaching-still-has-diversity-problem (accessed 15 December 2023).

Lyonette, C., Atfield, G., Barnes, S. and Owen, D. (2016) *Teachers' pay and equality: Online survey and qualitative study* [Online]. Available at https://wrap.warwick.ac.uk/79225/ (accessed 15 December 2023).

Miller, P. (2015) 'Perceived barriers to progression in UK universities: Preliminary findings from an exploratory study', *IIEP Policy Forum on Planning Higher Education Integrity*, Paris, 18–20.

Miller, P. (2016) 'White sanction, institutional, group and individual interaction in the promotion and progression of Black and minority ethnic academics and teachers in England', *Power & Education*, 8(3), 205–221.

Oberholzer, L. (2019) *Developing future Black Minority, Ethnic (BME) leader's self-efficacy through mentoring and coaching* [Online]. Available at: www.bameednetwork.com/wp-content/uploads/2019/11/CollectivED-Working-Papers.pdf (accessed 15 December 2023).

Pizarro, M. and Kohli, R. (2020) '"I stopped sleeping": Teachers of color and the impact of racial battle fatigue', *Urban Education*, 55(7), 967–991.

Tereshchenko, A., Mills, M. and Bradbury, A. (2020) Making progress? Employment and retention of BAME teachers in England. London: UCL Institute of Education [Online]. Available at: at: https://discovery.ucl.ac.uk/id/eprint/10117331/1/IOE_Report_BAME_Teachers.pdf (accessed 2 February 2024).

Wallace, D. (2020) 'The diversity trap? Critical explorations of black male teachers' negotiations of leadership and learning in London state schools', *Race Ethnicity and Education*, 23(3), 345–366.

Weale, S. (2021) 'Only 5% of state school governors in England from ethnic minorities – report', *The Guardian*, 29 June [Online]. Available at: www.theguardian.com/education/2021/jun/29/only-5-of-state-school-governors-in-england-from-ethnic-minorities-report (accessed 15 December 2023).

Wilkins, C. and Lall, R. (2011) 'You've got to be tough and I'm trying: Black and minority ethnic student teachers' experiences of initial teacher education', *Race Ethnicity and Education*, 14(3), 365–386.

WomenEd (2021) 'Daring to be different', *YouTube* [Online]. Available at: https://youtu.be/uqqo-bKC8ac?si (accessed 15 December 2023).

CASE STUDY 2

FITTING INTO THE MOULD

DO YOU HAVE TO CHANGE WHO YOU ARE?

Dr Joyce I-Hui Chen

Born and raised in Taiwan, I was taught to value humility and silence as virtues. However, these Asian ideals proved to be obstacles to my self-belief and career growth. When I moved to London, my enthusiasm for British culture was unmatched, but in a rural town dominated by homogeneity, I faced challenges trying to conform to their mould. Instead of celebrating my cultural roots, I hid them, feeling inadequate.

In hindsight, I was one of the few Asians in the community, unknowingly grappling with intersectional bias. Struggling to fit in, I experienced discomfort, not only in verbal interactions but also in non-verbal gestures. My quiet nature was mistaken for politeness, leading to being talked over and dismissed despite my hard work being recognised.

It was not until becoming a mother and starting my PhD study in 2017 that I confronted my conflicting cultural identities and values, recognising the barrier to true belonging which was trying to change who I am to be accepted (Brown, 2018). Later, I attended an eye-opening workshop on intersectionality by the Women Leadership Network (WLN) which revealed the complexities and bias that we face in the society.

I tried so hard to change myself to be accepted in a different culture and, in doing so, I lost myself. This revelation became the motivation for me to re-evaluate my values and identities. I started sharing and talking more about my cultural roots and their positive impact on myself and the communities. I talked about and created resources for colleagues and learners to understand what intersectionality means and how it impacts on us all. I am an advocate to support and mentor friends and colleagues who feel marginalised.

In this journey, I found the courage to stand tall, embracing change while preserving my values. Instead of fitting into a mould, we should break the mould and (re)shape our own path of belonging, one paved with authenticity and self-empowerment.

Reference

Brown, B. (2018) *Dare to Lead*. London: Penguin Random House.

CASE STUDY 3
THE F WORD
FAILURE
Angela Schofield

I absolutely agree that failure is a learning moment and, sometimes, it's important to acknowledge that the reality is you did fail.

I had an awful first term as a newly qualified teacher (NQT). I resigned in week 5 as I knew I couldn't continue. The comment on my NQT end-of-term report said, 'Despite failing this term, Angela still wants to try and pursue a teaching career'. The surprise on my mentor's face when I said I intended to carry on teaching destroyed the very last bit of confidence I had. There's no nice way of putting it, I failed, and I failed completely.

I think in part it was my lack of understanding of the formal hierarchical nature of the work environment in schools. I asked the Head of Maths if I could observe him teaching to support my development and was reported to the Head. Even though I'd organised events for a living, managed staff and budgets and statutory compliance in my first career, when I suggested ideas, I was told I needed to have more experience in school. I wasn't expected to contribute to discussions about trips or projects, for example. The comments included 'overfamiliar' and 'you speak as if you're on the same level'. By the end of the first month, I was incredibly insecure, which only made the situation worse. I avoided voicing opinions and was then seen as 'disengaged' and 'not committed'.

It was as if my personal background was not accepted as I didn't fit a preconceived view of an NQT. I don't think it was anyone's intention, but there was a lack of interest in my skills from my previous career and I was in a status-driven environment which was completely alien to me. The diverse experience I brought was not accepted by the homogeneous community I joined and I left after a month, feeling a failure.

After a few days in another school through an agency I was asked to commit full time for the rest of the year. The school then went into special measures so they couldn't employ NQTs. The week before transition day, I was asked to complete my NQT year but on supply. I knew I was only there because other people hadn't applied. I still felt I wasn't good enough.

So now to the most important people in my story – the women who picked me up, mentored me and put me back on track. A new Principal, Wendy Baxter, was simply the most inspiring and empowering woman I'd ever worked for. I was Head of Year by this time – a steep learning curve, but I thrived. I learned a lot and made many mistakes, but Wendy had a new approach. She had a mantra of *fearlessly failing faster*. When you fail, you learn, the more you fail the more you learn, the quicker you fail the quicker you learn. Failures were literally celebrated across the school. I don't think anyone failed faster than me, but what I've realised is that failing, when you are supported and encouraged, is very different from failing when you feel completely worthless.

The second woman I must thank is Hazel Pulley of Excelsior MAT. I met her when I moved schools, and she has supported me ever since. I still fail fast and fearlessly and, fortunately, Hazel has a very similar attitude to Wendy. Hazel told me that she was here to support me. She expected intentions to be good, and commitment to be high, but she did not expect me to be perfect. She is the inclusive, compassionate leader I strive to be now. We must celebrate diversity in its fullest sense and support and mentor all women to be the best they can be.

I want to be the woman who fixes another woman's crown without telling anyone else that it was crooked.

PART III

DISRUPTING THE GENDER PAY GAP FOR WOMEN LEADERS

INTRODUCTION

Vivienne Porritt

The authors in this section share the full inequity faced by women leaders globally in terms of the pay and conditions they experience. I often describe this as the education sector's dirty secret as it wasn't until WomenEd started talking, writing and being furious about this gap that most women even knew it existed. It does exist and it is getting worse every year. Thank you to our authors who are helping to expose this and we can all work collaboratively to reduce the inequity.

We see the gender pay gap in the salaries women leaders earn, in the lack of respect shown to them and the bias demonstrated when the colour of a woman's skin or her background means she is paid less for the exact same role as men. We also see the shocking gap in the pensions they accrue:

> Women's private pension pots in Great Britain are typically worth 35% less than those of their male colleagues by the time they reach 55, according to the first major government study into what has been termed 'the great gender pension chasm'. (Brignall, 2023)

One challenge for us now is to know the pension gap for public sector workers.

The fact that the gender pay gap is a global issue, as outlined by Liz Free, shows bias and discrimination on an industrial scale. This bias is interlinked as the paucity of development opportunities for women, as described by Katrina Kelly, contributes to the pay gap. We must draw on the WomenEd value of Challenge and disrupt this inequity in these ways:

- we must challenge ourselves and other individuals such as senior leaders and chief executive officers (CEOs) – get comfortable with negotiating, as Jenetta Hurst insists
- stop filling in the question about current salary or you are contributing to your own lower salary
- take Sue Prickett's advice and ask the senior leaders, governors and trustees of your organisation, 'why isn't our gender pay gap improving?'
- share these chapters with the women across your organisation so it becomes a dirty and very well-known issue
- lobby your organisation for pay transparency which 'builds trust and any relationship, including a working relationship, lasts longer when it is built on a foundation of trust' (Kaleen, 2022: 46)

- challenge the patriarchal systems that Abigail Mann rails against. Write to the leaders of your town, region, country and ask for their support to reduce the gap and hold them to account for this.

(See: https://womened.com/gender-pay-gap-campaign)

References

Brignall, M. (2023) 'Women's private pensions worth 35% less than men's in Great Britain', *The Guardian*, 5 June [Online]. Available at: www.theguardian.com/business/2023/jun/05/womens-private-pensions-gap-worth-less-than-mens-great-britain (accessed 25 January 2024).

Kaleen, R. (2022) *A Case of the Mondays*. Gorleston: Rethink Press.

14

SYSTEMIC SEXISM

THE GLOBAL GENDER PAY GAP

Liz Free

KEY POINTS

This chapter will explore the following topics:

- sadly, the global gender pay gap in education persists and we need local, national and global action to address this
- educational institutions should prioritise transparency in salary structures and promote accountability in compensation decisions
- further efforts should be made to promote equal access to leadership roles and career advancement opportunities for all educators
- promoting inclusive practices can contribute to the reduction of the gender pay gap
- at a systemic level, organisations and institutions have a moral, ethical and financial duty of care to understand, review and make concerted efforts to close the gender pay gap.

Introduction

The global gender pay gap has been a topic of concern and discussion for decades. Since the foundation of WomenEd in 2015, much work has been done across the WomenEd networks to highlight inequities in pay, to consider why these issues are important and to shine a light on ways in which we can close the gap within education. This work is required in order to recognise the contribution of women and to realise the potential of women for the benefit of education and wider society. And yet, many inequities for gender parity continue to pervade our profession.

We can look at the gender pay gap as a specific aspect of inequity and, through this chapter, I will explore how this inequality is manifested on a global scale. I will argue that the global gender pay gap in education is a symptom of inherent bias and systemic sexism, which is evident in systems and institutions throughout the world. I will consider some of the causes and possible actions we can take to close, and eliminate, the gap.

Firstly, we need to understand why the gender pay gap is an indicator of inherent systemic sexism. *The SAGE Encyclopedia of Psychology and Gender* (2017) defines institutional sexism as when institutional practices 'derive from systemic sexist beliefs that women are inferior to and therefore less capable than men. An example of institutional sexism is the differential pay rate between men and women' (Nadal, 2017: 941).

While progress has been made in various sectors, the education sector continues to grapple with significant disparities. One of WomenEd's four key aims is to reduce the gender pay gap and we would love to eradicate it completely across education. Through understanding the causes, implications and possible solutions more, we hope to foster a greater understanding and inspire actions and change that promote equality and equity within the educational landscape.

Understanding the Gender Pay Gap in Education

The gender pay gap refers to the difference in earnings between men and women. It is important to acknowledge that the gender pay gap is influenced by several factors, including societal norms, occupational segregation and systemic biases. These factors interact in complex ways, resulting in disparities in pay and opportunities.

I will explore this further through three key causes of the global gender pay gap:

1   Occupational segregation
2   Stereotyping and bias
3   Under-representation of women in education leadership.

Occupational segregation in the education sector exhibits patterns of occupational difference, with women often over-represented in lower-paying roles, such as professional services, early years and primary school teachers, while men dominate higher-paying positions, such as high school leaders, professors or administrators.

The proportional bias of the teaching profession by gender has remained consistent for decades. In Organisation for Economic Co-operation and Development (OECD) countries, the share of female teachers at primary level was 83% in 2010 and 2020, and about 64% in 2010 to 63% in 2020 at secondary level (OECD, 2022). In the USA women make up 89% of teachers at public elementary schools and 60% at public high schools (USAFacts, 2020). In China, 71% of primary teachers are female and 56% of senior school teachers are female (Sohu.com, 2021). There is a bias towards feminisation of the earlier years education profession throughout the world, with Saudi Arabia and Sub-Saharan Africa being some of the very few exceptions.

In many countries primary teachers are on a lower pay scale than secondary teachers. For example, six European countries have statutory starting salaries that are higher for secondary teachers than for pre-primary and primary teachers (Spain, France, Italy, Luxembourg, the Netherlands and Turkey) (European Commission/EACEA/Eurydice, 2022). In Belgium, the statutory starting salary is the same for pre-primary, primary and lower secondary teachers, while upper secondary teachers earn more. If we take into account pre-schools, over 12 European countries pay their pre-school teachers less (although certification is often of an equivalent academic standard). This occupational segregation and approaches to pay inherently bias against women as the highest proportion of women educators are found within the early and primary years, which is also a social bias reflected in leadership.

Alongside and parallel to occupational segregation, we see stereotyping and bias having a contributing effect. Gender stereotypes and biases continue to affect hiring, promotion, and salary decisions within the education sector. An example of this is the view that the age of the student is a determining factor of the quality and value of the teacher in terms of pay, thereby perpetuating the idea that early years and primary teachers are 'worth less'. Unconscious, and sometimes conscious, biases may lead to the undervaluation of women's skills and contributions, further exacerbating pay disparities.

Marta Encinas-Martín (2023) states,

> Historically, teaching has been one of the few skilled professions that has been accessible for women because it closely fitted the traditional stereotype of women as caregivers of children. While such gender stereotypes are less prevalent today than they were a few decades ago in many OECD countries, they might still be an important reason for the high share of female teachers, particularly at lower levels of education.

Encinas-Martín (2023) goes on to state that 'child rearing responsibilities still fall predominantly on women's shoulders'.

Despite initiatives for greater gender equity over the years, teaching remains a feminised profession with almost 80% of the workforce in OECD countries being women. This is representative of most countries. How is it therefore possible that there could be a gender pay gap?

The Council for International Schools collects annual data from international schools across the world. In 2022 they published an analysis that found in 2020:

- males earn on average 8,500 USD more than females
- white leaders earn on average 17,000 USD more than non-white leaders
- internationally hired heads earn on average 33,000 USD more than locally hired heads. (Neyra and Taverner, 2022)

Sadly, in 2021 the salary gaps were still evident and larger than in 2020 and, as the data above shows, demonstrates discrimination in terms of ethnicity and the local workforce.

In the UK, not only do significant gaps remain, but, as was observed by CIS in the international school sector, some are even increasing (Martin, 2022; 2023). In 2022, the gap for secondary school leaders had increased by a significant 37%. Vivienne Porritt, chair and global strategic leader of WomenEd, said, in response to the UK pay gap data, that it 'signals to women leaders that "teaching is not an equitable profession"' (Walker, 2022).

Not only do we see continued occupational segregation within the profession along-side a persistent gender pay gap, there is also a lack of female leadership in education with an under-representation of women in leadership positions. The numbers remain staggeringly sad. In America's public schools, women represented 68.6% percent of all principals in elementary schools, 43.7% of middle school principals and only 35.5% percent of high school principals (Taie and Lewis, 2022). This proportional representation is far below the percentage of female teachers in each education phase.

In the UK, a similar picture is emerging. The Department for Education in the UK concluded that 'Female teachers are less likely than their male counterparts to be in leadership positions (head teachers, deputy heads, assistant heads), however this difference is reducing over time' (Gov.uk, 2023). In 2022/23, 69% of teachers on the wider leadership scale were female, up from 66% in 2010/11. This compares to 77% of classroom teachers being female in 2022/23 and 76% in 2010/11. An improvement, but far too slow for this and especially for the next generation of the profession.

At this pace, it will take three to four decades to see true equitable representation. And this remains a problem, not only for moral and ethical purposes but also in ensuring the right people are at the right table when systemic, strategic decisions are being made, especially regarding promotions and remuneration. Ginsberg famously said, 'Women belong in all places where decisions are being made' (Mears, 2009). Women's limited access to senior leadership roles restricts their ability to influence decision-making processes and advocate for equitable compensation, representation and voice. Ensuring a comprehensive understanding of the imperative for a gender equitable global profession must be a priority for all education leaders and policy influencers.

Implications of the Gender Pay Gap

Creating a sense of urgency to address the gender pay gap as a visible and tangible consequence of a systemically sexist profession is important. So, why does closing the gender pay gap in education matter? Making a case for gender equality is a moral, social and economic imperative. The implications of such a gap affect every aspect of education, society and community:

- *Economic inequality*: The gender pay gap perpetuates economic inequality, as women's lower earnings impact their income alongside the long-term implications of lower pensions. This limits women's financial independence and exacerbates the cycle of gender financial inequity (such gender discrimination and inequity is illegal in many countries). In addition, 'in the poorest countries in the world, more than 40 percent of female qualified jobs are teachers' (Le Nestour and Moscoviz, 2020). Any pay gap in such systems has a significant local and national impact for women and wider society.

- *Career aspirations and role models*: The gender pay gap in education can discourage female students and early career teachers from pursuing careers in academia or educational leadership. The lack of visible female role models in higher-paying positions may limit their aspirations and perpetuate a cycle of under-representation.
- *Talent drain*: Inequitable compensation practices can result in the loss of talented female educators who seek better opportunities in other sectors. The education system loses valuable expertise, leading to a potential decline in overall quality and lack of representation where systemic and strategic decisions are being made, thereby slowing progress and perpetuating the gender divide.

Addressing the Gender Pay Gap in Education

Acknowledging the issues and putting in place direct action to address the gender pay gap is an imperative for everyone, at a granular local level through to national and international practices. Everyone can have an impact and I strongly encourage all readers of this book to think about what action they can take within their roles to work towards the following:

- *Pay transparency and accountability*: Educational institutions should prioritise transparency in salary structures and promote accountability in compensation decisions. Regular audits and reporting mechanisms can help identify and rectify pay disparities. In the European Union and Switzerland, the 2023 Pay Transparency Directive includes a set of binding measures to increase pay transparency (Thoma, 2023).
- *Equalising opportunities*: Efforts should be made to promote equal access to leadership roles and career advancement opportunities for all educators. Mentorship programmes, training initiatives and unbiased promotion processes can help dismantle barriers and foster gender equity, equality and representation.
- *Changing perceptions and stereotypes*: Raising awareness about unconscious biases and promoting inclusive practices can contribute to the reduction of the gender pay gap. This includes research-informed training for all those in education human resources and those involved in recruitment (Porritt et al., 2021). It also extends to encouraging diverse representations of gender in all aspects of education, including curricula, teacher training resources and leadership programmes that will challenge traditional gender roles and stereotypes.

- *Policies and legislation*: Governments and educational bodies, such as accreditation organisations, should enact and enforce legislation/requirements that address gender pay gaps. This can include mandates for pay equity, mandatory reporting of data, gender-neutral job recruitment and evaluation processes, and penalties for non-compliant institutions. As individuals we can encourage these organisations to take proactive action, and celebrate those that are visibly taking action.

Disruptions

- The global gender pay gap in education persists as a complex issue with far-reaching implications. To bridge this gap, it is crucial to address the underlying causes, such as occupational segregation, biases, discrimination and limited female representation in leadership roles.
- Through efforts such as pay transparency, equalising opportunities, changing perceptions and implementing supportive policies, the education sector can work towards creating a more equitable environment for educators, and for the communities that these educators lead and serve. Our WomenEd campaign has detailed advice: https://womened.com/gender-pay-gap-campaign.
- Achieving gender pay parity in education will benefit individuals and contribute to broader social and economic progress.
- By prioritising equity, equality and representation at all levels of education, we can build a brighter future for all learners and educators worldwide.

References

Encinas-Martín, M. (2023) *Gender differences in career expectations and feminisation of the teaching profession*. Available at: www.oecd-ilibrary.org/sites/4aa4d2f7-en/index. html?itemId=/content/component/4aa4d2f7-en (accessed 20 January 2024).

European Commission/EACEA/Eurydice (2022) *Teachers' and School Heads' Salaries and Allowances in Europe – 2020/2021*. Luxembourg: Publications Office of the European Union.

Gov.UK (2023) *School workforce in England, reporting year 2022* [Online]. Available at: https://explore-education-statistics.service.gov.uk/find-statistics/school-workforce-in-england (accessed 15 July 2023).

Le Nestour, A. and Moscoviz, L. (2020) *Six things you should know about female teachers* [Blog]. [Online]. Available at: www.cgdev.org/blog/six-things-you-should-know-about-female-teachers (accessed 16 July 2023).

Martin, M. (2022) 'Secondary head Gender pay gap widens by over a third', *Tes Magazine*, 20 November [Online]. Available at: www.tes.com/magazine/news/general/secondary-head-gender-pay-gap-widens-over-third (accessed 16 July 2023).

Martin, M. (2023) 'Female teachers "work 81 days a year for free", *Tes*, 23 February [Online]. Available at: https://www.tes.com/magazine/news/general/gender-pay-gap-education-teaching-women-work-free (accessed 16 July 2023).

Mears, B. (2009) *Justice Ginsburg ready to welcome Sotomayor* [Online]. Available at: https://edition.cnn.com/2009/POLITICS/06/16/sotomayor.ginsburg/index.html (accessed 2 November 2023).

Nadal, K. L. (2017) *The SAGE Encyclopaedia of Psychology and Gender*. Thousand Oaks, CA: SAGE.

Neyra, A. and Taverner, K. (2022) *Head of school salary research tells a new story* [Online]. Available at: www.cois.org/about-cis/news/post/~board/perspectives-blog/post/head-of-school-salary-research-tells-a-new-story (accessed 15 July 2023).

Organisation for Economic Co-operation and Development (OECD) (2022) *Education at a glance 2022: OECD indicators* [Online]. Available at: www.oecd-ilibrary.org/education/education-at-a-glance-2022_3197152b-en (accessed 20 January 2024).

Porritt, V., Hannay, L. and Plummer, P. (2021) *Deliberate disruption: Issues of gender and diversity* [Online]. Available at: https://my.chartered.college/impact_article/deliberate-disruption-issues-of-gender-and-diversity/ (accessed 20 January 2024).

Sohu.com (2021) *On the other hand, the proportion of male teachers in primary and secondary schools is declining year by year* [Online]. Available at: www.sohu.com/a/491888517_617954 (accessed 15 July 2023).

Taie, S. and Lewis, L. (2022) *Characteristics of 2020–21 public and private K–12 school principals* [Online]. Available at: https://nces.ed.gov/pubs2022/2022112.pdf (accessed 15 July 2023).

Thoma, C. K. (2023) *How to best prepare for the recently adopted EU directive on pay transparency?* [Online]. Available at: www.ey.com/en_ch/workforce/how-to-best-prepare-for-the-recently-adopted-eu-directive-on-pay-transparency (accessed 2 November 2023).

USAFacts (2020) 'Who are the nation's 4 million teachers?', *USAFacts*, 14 December [Online]. Available at: https://usafacts.org/articles/who-are-the-nations-4m-teachers/ (accessed 15 July 2023).

Walker, A (2022) 'Gender pay gap widening for school leaders, new analysis shows', *Schools Week*, 20 November [Online]. Available at: https://schoolsweek.co.uk/gender-pay-gap-widening-for-school-leaders-new-analysis-shows/ (accessed 15 July 2023).

15

DISRUPTING THE GENDER PAY GAP

EMPOWERING FEMALE MIDDLE LEADERS TO PROGRESS INTO SENIOR LEADERSHIP

Katrina Kerry

KEY POINTS

This chapter will:

- show why the gender pay gap needs to be disrupted in the education sector
- give practical guidance on how to build confidence in women to disrupt the gap
- challenge school leaders to support progression of female middle leaders through collaboration and empowerment across a multi-academy trust.

Introduction

The gender pay gap is an ethical problem that continues to be a global issue. Over the past 30 years the gender pay gap has slowly reduced across all sectors in general, yet despite this, we still see a large and growing gap in the education sector, including the organisation this research project is focused within, a multi-academy trust of nine secondary schools. I am exploring the reasons why this could be and what recommendations could be shared that could potentially reduce or close this gap within the specific organisation and across education in the future. Specifically, I sought the views of female middle leaders on promotion to senior leadership positions and explored what can be done to support females' career progression to secure senior leadership posts in the future and contribute to reducing the gender pay gap.

The Size of the Gap

There is robust literature available concerning the gender pay gap in education. Notable works include Fairfax (2018) and Bertrand and Hallock (2001). In *Closing the Gender Pay Gap in Education: A Leadership Imperative* (2022), the collaboration between ASCL, NAHT, nga and WomenEd drew on the data from the Department for Education's 2021 Workforce Census and undoubtedly establishes there is a gender pay gap for women leaders in schools in England which increases each year within schools and trusts. Consequently, the Department for Education's advice to the School Teachers Pay and Conditions Board (2022) cited 'Closing the gender pay gap in education: A leadership imperative' (ibid.) when stating,

> during the period from 2010 to 2020, there was a pay gap between male and female teachers once leadership grades were included in the analysis. The pay gap averaged 4% of full-time female teachers' base pay, and 3% for part-time.

However, as ASCL et al. (2022) established, it is the gap in pay at leadership levels that is significant. The divergence point is at age 35–39, with the difference between average salaries between men and women almost doubling from age 35–39 to age 40–44. The difference by age 60 and over for Headteachers reached an average of a staggering £15,961 in 2021 data.

By November 2023, the data showed 'the pay gap between female and male head teachers is the largest in 12 years, with women this year earning £3,908 less on average than their male counterparts' (ASCL et al., 2023).

Ryan et al. (2016) refers to the glass ceiling causing difficulties for women, and this is something the research organisation is enthusiastic about addressing. The topic is of vital importance in the current climate in education as a higher level of gender equity needs to be promoted and achieved in this sector.

It is also clear that we need data regarding the ethnicity pay gap in education.

> Our report Closing the Gender Pay Gap in Education: A leadership imperative, … highlights the challenges for women, including women of colour, and stresses the need for greater information on the pay penalties that people from different ethnic backgrounds working in education may face. (Janes, 2022)

Smith-Carrier et al. (2021) implies that addressing the gap in salary by gender is not enough as it substantially underestimates the long-term breadth and depth of barriers for females with many other factors requiring consideration. Potential social factors include:

- confidence to apply for promotion
- wellbeing
- family dynamics
- maternity leave and motherhood
- bias and discrimination.

It is evident from the existing research that women are disadvantaged compared to their male colleagues throughout their careers as well as the impact on their pension (ASCL et al., 2022), and employers would benefit from the recommendations drawn from the inferences in my research.

The Research Study

Ten women working in middle leadership roles across a multi-academy trust of nine secondary schools in the East Midlands, England were interviewed.

This research study investigated the gender pay gap in the education sector and explored how more female middle leaders can be empowered to progress into senior leadership roles to narrow the gender pay gap.

This is in the context of my multi-academy trust when our gender pay gap in 2021 showed that women in the median (middle) group were paid 32 pence lower *per hour* than men for every pound earned in 2021–22.

Think that through and work it out, based on 35 hours a week multiplied by 32 pence over a year. What is it about your male colleagues that makes them worth more than you?

The ten participants were females aged between 25 and 45 years old, working in middle leadership roles across a multi-academy trust of nine secondary schools. Existing female middle leaders were the target group as they have progressed from teaching posts by applying and being successful at interview for their current roles. Each interview contained the same semi-structured questions, allowing me to extend on their answers if participants made points that required further exploration. As the method of data collection was 1:1 semi-structured interviews, the analysis was thematic as this is a useful tool for analysing qualitative data.

The participants' transcripts were anonymised with responses from the qualitative questions discussed during semi-structured interviews with all ten participants. Each of the participant responses from the individual interview questions were coded from the patterns found. This coding was used to create topical themes across the discussions as suggested by Marshall and Rossman (1989).

Although the participants came from a limited subsample within the organisation, they hold a wide variety of different middle leadership roles across the organisation. The interview began by asking the participants about the experiences they had had within their career, giving them the opportunity to talk about previous development, appointments and promotions during their tenure at various stages building up to this point in their careers.

The positive effect of the National Professional Qualification for Middle Leadership (NPQML) had impacted upon participants' confidence and level of understanding in applying for their current roles. One participant said, 'it has provided me with the skills to create and implement whole school policies' and another said, 'it is helping to develop my confidence too'.

One participant said they had originally wanted to become a pastoral leader but having a curriculum role allowed her to 'utilise my passion to better our students'. Another participant said,

> my personal passion has always been in closing that pupil premium gap and finding ways to bring as many possibilities and opportunities for those students as possible. My current middle leadership role should allow this passion to become a reality.

Senior Leadership Team (SLT) roles were mentioned by many participants, including one saying, 'I would like to move into a SLT role, perhaps in curriculum'. New multi-academy trust (MAT) central roles were also clearly of interest to participants, with one woman wanting to progress to a role 'trust wide where not only do you get to work alongside people, but you get to support people in their journeys too'.

Participants also talked about their future ambitions to secure leadership roles in a different setting, for example, being on the SLT in a Special School setting.

One candidate did say that she did not want to apply for further promotion because she currently enjoyed her role and was reluctant to take the risk of gaining a new position she may not enjoy as much: 'It is really important to me that I am happy in my career and that I'm doing a job that makes me happy.' One participant said she wanted 'time to make sure that I am doing the best I can in my current role before looking at progression'.

Maternity leave was raised by one participant stating that 'If I wanted to have kids, I would not apply for something, but I've learned to realise that shouldn't affect my capability if I wanted to apply for a job'. Although this individual is stating they would not be put off applying for promotion, it is clear from the literature that would not be the case in all organisations, therefore it can still be a perceived barrier for women wanting to progress. 'The concept of a "motherhood penalty" refers to the decline in income, perceived competence, and chance for career progression that comes after a working woman has children' (Becker, 2019: paragraph 3).

Opportunities for shadowing were proposed as a good opportunity to gain insight from other staff in the MAT who are already in the key posts female participants would consider to be their next role, with one participant suggesting this could 'help me to see my skills in a new light'.

In addition, women wanted opportunities to collaborate across schools within the trust. One participant suggested that 'Across the trust and into other trusts outside of that as well, I think that's the tangible way to allow me personally to progress'.

The three key themes that emerged from our discussions were:

- support to further empower women leaders
- enhanced professional development
- opportunities to collaborate.

The level of success in reducing the gender pay gap in education is still very much subject to the culture of the organisation and its desire to take on the problem-solving approach to combating the problem.

Given the previous evidence from the literature review, the gender pay gap data and the responses to the interview questions, there is a strong case for the implementation of specific recommendations for employers to support their female employees to aspire to achieve further promotion within their careers. Having the confidence to negotiate their worth and having opportunities to be professionally developed and mentored well are options not available to all women in education. To describe these as necessary disruptions highlights a lack of equitable treatment for women leaders. In addition, it is important to recognise what the group from the research suggested is already supporting them on their journeys, citing shadowing, opportunities to work collaboratively and visiting other schools which has been helpful in supporting them to grow.

Recommendations

The gender pay gap in schools and across education will not close by itself. There are clear strategies identified in this research, and the previous research of others, that can reduce the gender pay gap in education over time. The recommendations detail what organisations can do to support individual women and their workforce holistically and demonstrate equitable, inclusive leadership.

Provide opportunities to shadow colleagues

Shadowing is a known development technique that can be highly effective when used in an educational context. Peer learning enables a leader to observe a colleague over a set period to see how they operate in a naturalistic setting. Any period of shadowing can be advantageous in building knowledge and understanding of the observed context/ subject. However, it is suggested the optimum period may be between one day and a one-month period. In an educational setting a female middle leader may benefit from observing a current senior leader at different points throughout the academic year as some elements of the leader's role would be fulfilled periodically. For example, the creation of a whole-school timetable is created in the summer term and an aspiring leader could not observe this in action in the autumn or spring term.

Provide opportunities for secondments or volunteering to retain talent within the organisation

Boeddeker (2010) suggests leadership that focuses on supporting teachers' professional and emotional needs is successful in reducing attrition rates. Morgan (2017) advocates Talent Management that enables employers to retain effective employees by giving them compelling experiences in their roles. Dobele et al. (2014) highlight the challenges of aspiring leaders' heavy teaching timetables and advocates secondments as an effective way of navigating through this potential barrier of losing quality staff.

One participant I interviewed spoke passionately about volunteering to mentor student teachers before they became a middle leader, stating, 'the trainee teachers I've worked with are now established members of the English team. One has even participated in a leadership training course to develop her own career which I'm enormously proud of having been her mentor'.

Create a psychologically safe environment where women can thrive

Pyke (2013) describes organisational culture as 'pivotal' as it alleviates the negative impact of any lack of support in the work environment, and staff can thrive. Robinson (2024) cited a Statista report showing the average Women's Empowerment Index (WEI) global score is 0.607, so women are only empowered to achieve 60% of their full potential. Page Executive (n.d.) highlights that 'organisations which lack psychologically safe environments produce fewer female leaders, develop their female workers less effectively, and consequently experience worse outcomes', particularly for women from underrepresented groups.

Check access to development opportunities is proportionate in terms of gender distribution and uptake

Research suggests men are more likely to have the confidence to ask for development. Niederle and Vesterlund (2007) state that 'women shy away from competition and men embrace it'. Employers would benefit from checking the ratios of male and female employees in middle leadership positions and try to maintain these ratios when these colleagues are recommended for further leadership training. For example, if 70% of middle leaders are female, 70% of the workforce at middle leadership level should be offered and take up development opportunities.

Offer women enhanced support when returning from maternity leave

Organisations can provide return to work strategies that recognise the issues faced by women. Corrente et al. (2022) refer to a need to consider how one should assess gender differences in psychological factors. Santos (2016) also urges employers to consider how female staff may be feeling at times when their employment hinders their ability to observe their children growing up, and how they could support female staff who may experience stress from this. Sheppard and Campbell (2023) state that,

> According to the Government Equalities Office, there are larger pay penalties due to taking time out of work for maternity leave and moving to part-time work in order to manage the competing demands of work and families.

Champion flexible working and celebrate this publicly

Coalter (2018) suggests job advertisements that cite flexible working as an opportunity for prospective candidates now attract 20% more applications. Offering women as much flexibility in their working patterns as possible enables them to balance the other commitments in their lives, including motherhood. Also, employers can be clear that even the most senior posts welcome applications from candidates wanting part-time working hours. Cotton and Gresty (2007) are advocates for the use of the internet: in modern times employees have more opportunities to work in a more remote way, generating greater levels of flexibility in working patterns through enhancements within digital technology. This is supported by Santos (2016), who identifies the struggles of mothers trying to juggle the demands of children alongside work in progressing throughout their careers. In opposition, Padavic et al. (2020) suggest 'flexibility stigma' can arise when women take advantage of flexible working offers which can exacerbate gender inequality through a perception of unfairness towards other colleagues.

Mentoring through a collaborative and nurturing approach

Mentoring and coaching are both highly effective ways of developing staff. Emelo (2015) defines mentoring as the ability to gain new understanding, developed through knowledge of other colleagues which suggests people can collaborate and learn from one another across varying roles and locations. A good mentor can capably support their mentee to go for promotion by identifying the level of ability they possess and supporting them to feel enabled to do so. Organisations would be wise to advocate collaborative mentorship for staff that could be considered for promotion, giving them the opportunity to collaborate with a colleague in a developmental capacity that is not currently their line manager. Kirchmeyer (2005) advocates the clear professional developmental benefits to career success attained from effective mentoring.

This research and its impact upon the participants is a further step towards understanding how the work environment should support female colleagues in securing promotion to senior leadership roles, whilst still supporting their wellbeing and work–life balance. Collectively maximising participants' opportunities to be successful in promotions will support reduction of the gender pay gap within the organisation in years to come.

I have learned:

- that there is evidently a gender pay gap in the education sector across all organisations globally
- women are the dominant gender working in the education sector, but despite this they do not hold a representative ratio of the higher-paid roles in educational establishments
- there are also gaps in pensions claimed by retired women that have worked in the education sector in comparison to their male colleagues.

This research and its impact upon the participants is a further step towards understanding how the work environment can potentially support female colleagues in securing promotion to senior leadership roles, whilst still supporting their wellbeing and work–life balance. Collectively maximising participants' opportunities to be successful in promotions will reduce the gender pay gap within the organisation in years to come.

Education organisations need to work with their female colleagues to address their lack of recognition, their inequitable remuneration, excessive workloads, perceived gender inequalities or family or health issues. I hope the recommendations from this research can guide organisations to offer appropriate support to women who want to progress in their leadership and be paid what they are worth.

Disruptions

- Ask about the size of the gender pay gap in your organisation and what leaders and governors/trustees are doing to reduce it.
- When you are offered a job, thank them, and say you accept *subject to salary* – this opens the negotiation process.
- Watch WomenEd's negotiation video at https://youtu.be/UTMeABj2dAg?si.
- Have the confidence to ask for and access the development opportunities that will support you to progress, including any potential shadowing or secondment opportunities that arise.
- Challenge your mentor/line manager to support you to achieve the next steps in your career.
- Develop new networks that will expose you to the experiences of others and open you up to new opportunities.

References

ASCL, NAHT, nga and WomenEd (2022) *Closing the gender pay gap in education: A leadership imperative* [Online]. Available at: https://www.ascl.org.uk/ASCL/media/ASCL/Our%20view/Campaigns/Closing-the-gender-pay-gap-in-Education-a-leadership-imperative.pdf (accessed 15 January 2024).

ASCL, NAHT, nga and WomenEd (2023) 'Gender pay gap for secondary heads widest for a decade, warn education organisations, on Equal Pay Day', *WomenEd*, 22 November [Online]. Available at: https://drive.google.com/file/d/1YZPMXvZdU5LkvWIS7-jtz1rvX0RZGB3n/view (accessed 20 January 2024).

Becker, S. (2019) 'The motherhood penalty: Why employers fear women', *Monash Business School*, 13 November [Online]. Available at: https://impact.monash.edu/labour-market/the-motherhood-penalty/ (accessed 20 January 2024).

Bertrand, M. and Hallock, K. F. (2001) 'The gender gap in top corporate jobs', *ILR Review*, 55(1), 3–21.

Boeddeker, J. C. (2010) A Comparison of Special Education Teachers' and Administrators' Perceptions of School Climate Factors Leading to Teacher Attrition. Doctoral dissertation, University of Nevada, Las Vegas.

Coalter, M. (2018) *Talent Architects: How to Make Your School a Great Place to Work.* London: Hachette.

Corrente, M., Ferguson, K. and Bourgeault, I. L. (2022) 'Mental health experiences of teachers: A scoping review', *Journal of Teaching and Learning*, 16(1), 23–43.

Cotton, D. R. E. and Gresty, K. A. (2007) 'The rhetoric and reality of e-learning: Using the think-aloud method to evaluate an online resource', *Assessment & Evaluation in Higher Education*, 32(5), 583–600.

Department for Education (2022) *Government evidence to the STRB* [Online]. Available at: https://assets.publishing.service.gov.uk/government/uploads/system/uploads/attachment_data/file/1060707/Government_evidence_to_the_STRB_2022.pdf (accessed 15 January 2024).

Dobele, A. R., Rundle-Thiele, S. and Kopanidis, F. (2014) 'The cracked glass ceiling: Equal work but unequal status', *Higher Education Research & Development*, 33(3), 456–468.

Emelo, R. (2015) *Modern Mentoring*. Alexandria, VA: ATD Press.

Fairfax, L. M. (2018) 'Fall 2018 Symposium: All on board: Board diversity trends reflect signs of promise and concern', *The George Washington Law Review*, 87, 1031.

Janes, W. (2022) 'Teachers' union calls on Government to address ethnicity pay gap', *Independent*, 8 January [Online]. Available at: www.independent.co.uk/news/uk/naht-asian-government-teachers-gender-pay-gap-b1989093.html (accessed 20 January 2024).

Kirchmeyer, C. (2005) 'The effects of mentoring on academic careers over time: Testing performance and political perspectives', *Human Relations*, 58(5), 637–660.

Marshall, C. and Rossman, G. B. (1989) *Designing Qualitative Research*. Thousand Oaks, CA: Sage.

Morgan, J. (2017) *The Employee Experience Advantage: How to Win the War for Talent by Giving Employees the Workspaces They Want, the Tools They Need, and a Culture They Can Celebrate.* Hoboken, NJ: John Wiley & Sons.

Niederle, M. and Vesterlund, L. (2007) 'Do women shy away from competition? Do men compete too much?', *The Quarterly Journal of Economics*, 122(3), 1067–1101.

Padavic, I., Ely, R. J. and Reid, E. M. (2020) 'Explaining the persistence of gender inequality: The work–family narrative as a social defence against the 24/7 work culture', *Administrative Science Quarterly*, 65(1), 61–111.

Page Executive (n.d.) *Why psychological safety is critical for gender equality in the workplace* [Online]. Available at: www.pageexecutive.com/advice/topics/diversity-inclusion/why-psychological-safety-is-critical-for-gender-equality-in-the-workplace (accessed 21 January 2024).

Pyke, J. (2013) 'Women, choice and promotion or why women are still a minority in the professoriate', *Journal of Higher Education Policy and Management*, 35(4), 444–454.

Robinson, C. (2024) 'Women's Empowerment Isn't Enough. Activating Women Is More Powerful' *Forbes*, 22 January [Online]. Available at: https://www.forbes.com/sites/cherylrobinson/2024/01/22/womens-empowerment-isnt-enough-activating-women-is-more-powerful/ (accessed 20 January 2024).

Ryan, M., Haslam, S.A, Morgenroth, T., Rink, F., Stoker, J. and Peters, K. (2016) 'Getting on top of the glass cliff: Reviewing a decade of evidence, explanations, and impact', *The Leadership Quarterly*, 27(3), 446–455.

Santos, G. G. (2016) 'Career barriers influencing career success: A focus on academics' perceptions and experiences', *Career Development International*, 21(1), 60–84.

Sheppard, E. and Campbell, G. (2023) 'We're on a road to nowhere: Women aged 30-39 – why are they the largest demographic to leave teaching every year?, *Chartered College of Teaching*, 31 January [Online]. Available at: https://my.chartered.college/impact_article/were-on-a-road-to-nowhere-women-aged-30-39-why-are-they-the-largest-demographic-to-leave-teaching-every-year/ (accessed 20 January 2024).

Smith-Carrier, T., Penner, M., Cecala, A. L. and Agócs, C. (2021) 'It's not just a pay gap: Quantifying the gender wage and pension gap at a post-secondary institution in Canada', *Canadian Journal of Higher Education/Revue canadienne d'enseignement supérieur*, 51(2), 74–84.

16

NEGOTIATING SALARIES

Jenetta Hurst

KEY POINTS

This chapter will:

- discuss the impact of the gender pay gap felt by women in education
- show how salary and remuneration package negotiations can disrupt the inequity in salaries
- show what is needed to prepare for negotiations.

Taking Positive Action to Achieve Equitable Salaries

This chapter provides actionable, powerful, and meaningful suggestions for tackling what can feel like a sensitive or challenging feature of the job interview – negotiating salaries. It outlines considerations around salary negotiations, personal preparedness, and the benefits for both the individual and school of securing the desired salary.

Against the backdrop of global financial strain and teacher shortages (*Tes*, 2023: 1), the recent pay awards in the UK (Whittaker, 2023: 21) are a real-terms pay decrease of 13% since 2010 in England (Sibeta, 2023: 4). This means the impact of the gender pay gap will continue to be felt by female teachers in the profession (*Tes*, 2023: 2).

Yet through positive action, women can empower themselves to achieve equitable salaries and negotiate remuneration packages that reflect their experience and years of service. Through an exploration of personal encounters and drawing on advice from numerous sources, we will look at the potential for positive change.

Talking points concerning closing the gender pay gap and entering into negotiations include:

- having your desired figure and personal needs in mind
- ensuring your qualifications pay you back
- researching and talking openly with trusted friends and colleagues about salaries if you feel comfortable to do so
- a willingness to walk away from the job offer.

Be Ambitious. Create Sisterhood.

In mid-2023 I was honoured to be a guest at a special event in London's Soho in celebration of the prestigious Ivor Novello Awards. This unique night was a precursor to the annual awards for the world's greatest songwriters. The CEO of Universal Music Publishing Group and the 'She Is' Music Mentorship Programme, Jody Gerson, took to the stage. Her message was clear: 'Be ambitious. Create sisterhood.'

Gerson spoke about the importance to women of telling our stories and went on to share memories of her childhood in Philadelphia, growing up in clubs surrounded by the most amazing Motown singers and producers.

The WomenEd values of *communication*, *confidence* and *community* were presented that evening, and shaped my thinking around this chapter on skills for negotiating salaries.

The Landscape

As an arts practitioner and, more specifically, a qualified secondary music specialist, it has always been somewhat of a challenge to keep up with the best financial offers available to teachers in the English educational workforce. I am a subject leader and also a leader of a foundation subject (a non-core subject) in England. Some might say that music and arts teachers offer a niche skillset, and this would be true. However, from the offset during my training year the inequity in the system was apparent. Music was not a 'shortage subject' and there was no financial incentive of a 'golden hello' as there was for my drama trainee colleagues on the postgraduate certificate in education (PGCE) route into teaching.

Entering the workforce as a Year 1 teacher-in-charge of my subject, I had no idea for some years that the introduction of Teaching and Learning Responsibility (TLR) payments on a scale would mean that Heads of Department of core subjects (for instance, English, Maths and Science) may typically be offered a higher value TLR and that how much this might be would vary from school to school. I accepted that this was the landscape that I existed within and continued with my work, glad of the opportunity to contribute to and work within varying school communities, overlooking the possibility of using the TLR as a means of salary negotiation.

It quickly became apparent that the best way to improve my salary would be to take up new opportunities in new schools with a bigger department and increased responsibility. This only suited me for so long. I soon discovered the true importance of community and belonging in schools and the value of growing with my team. Moving between schools was no longer a viable or desirable option for me.

Along the journey to senior leadership, a long, steady and at times slow journey, in a school community that was a great fit for me, I began to carve out clarity of the role I desired, which was developing teachers through effective continuing professional development and what was required to achieve this. In practice this looked like:

- demonstrating ability and a positive work ethic
- being open and responsive to feedback
- being a team player
- learning what motivates individuals and a range of strategies to offer support to staff
- investing in self-development in both time and finance.

To hold a strong position for negotiating, you must know your worth and what sets you apart from other potential applicants or team members. This often takes a little extra and could come in the form of participating actively in whole-school continuing professional development, taking advantage of external development offers such as the National Professional Qualifications suite on offer in England, or The Educational Collaborative for International Schools (https://www.ecis.org/), or by joining professional bodies, such as the Chartered College of Teaching, for their leadership programmes, networking and collegiality.

Some of the steps I took included the completion of various middle leader and senior leader development programmes, such as Equal Access to Promotion, Teaching Leaders, and my MA in Leadership. Importantly I also spoke openly with my superiors about aspirations for senior leadership, realising that my development seemed to be up to me. Women needing more qualifications is, however, an element in the inequity we face: 'They had deliberately undertaken these additional qualifications to be "the best qualified for the role" so no criticism could be levelled against them' (Choudry, 2019: 61).

I successfully negotiated increased responsibilities but accepted nominal increases in salary for these roles. At the time, the job title felt of more value to me than the remuneration, and experience is key to making those career next steps. Deciding to be more intentional about financial goals is crucial and something that became a personal consideration later for me. I eventually experienced securing a role where my Master's degree paid me back, before even having received the certificate and graduating. Finally, success!

Revisiting and Refining the Approach

Achieving success in negotiating a salary required a reflection on my qualifications, self-investment and track record on paper and was necessary to see my true value as a teacher and leader. Going into the job interview with a number in mind was key to securing that figure. As a dedicated listener of business podcasts such as David Shands and Donni Wiggins' *Social Proof,* and a follower of Bianca and Byron Cole's *Self-Made Network,* the importance of knowing your number is emphasised in their message. Towards the end of the interview, when asked whether you have any questions could be an opportunity to raise the matter of salary. You may not have a specific question to ask, but this is your opportunity to outline the level of salary you have in mind. Having the confidence to broach the topic of salary is crucial and something you may need to rehearse (indeed, 2023: 14). Equally, if you want the job when offered it, WomenEd advises you to say, 'Thank you, subject to salary', which opens the door to negotiation. After all, in no other sector would people accept a job without knowing the specific salary. It's very good to know that recent research shows '64% of women and 59% of men reported negotiating for promotions or better compensation' (Academy of Management Insights, n.d.) so the old stereotype that women don't ask may be changing. This can spur us all on to expect appropriate remuneration.

There are alternative schools of thought on this matter, with some advisors suggesting that it is best to wait until you are offered the role, before discussing salary (Academy of Management Insights, n.d.: 5; TesWorld, 2020). There are certainly no hard and fast rules here and your personal circumstance will likely lead your thought process and approach.

> Never be afraid to negotiate: The fear of rejection stops many people from negotiating. ... Always remember that negotiation is a two-way street, and the worst that can happen is that the other party says no, but the best-case scenario can lead to significant gains. (Lokenauth, 2023: 1–3)

In the specific example outlined above, as a female being interviewed by another female, I was pleased with the assertive, immediate response and the positive outcome of agreeing the desired salary within the range offered.

Of course, there may be instances when negotiations do not go in your favour. It is important to know when to conclude negotiations and to be willing to walk away from a job opportunity if the number you have in mind is non-negotiable for your personal circumstances (Half, 2023: 14; indeed, 2023: 14).

Widening Experience as a Tool to Negotiation

It is important to remember that negotiation at interview does not solely relate to salary and Teaching and Learning Responsibility payments. Perhaps you need flexibility around your working day, with time to accommodate childcare arrangements or specific training opportunities such as a financial contribution from your employer towards a qualification that will enhance your school-based role.

Skills developed outside of the classroom can also contribute to a strong negotiation. Perhaps you are a school governor or voluntary Board member or trustee for an external organisation. If you carry out consultancy work or tutor young people, write blogs and articles for publications, the skills you hold will be transferable and desirable to employers. Note all these skills down, prior to interview or your conversation to discuss salary, and communicate your wider offer and skillset with clarity, linking it to the work you are currently doing or hope to do in the future.

Impact of Negotiation

Taking the brave step of entering into negotiations can prove beneficial in several ways. Some advantages of achieving an agreement or desired salary for both employer and employee include:

- accommodating life circumstances and achieving a level of comfort
- feeling valued by your employer
- avoiding future feelings of resentment as an employee
- the school community benefitting from the discretionary effort of employees.

Not all employees will be motivated by money; nonetheless, there are other motivating factors that can be negotiated with staff. These are likely to encourage their commitment and increase the likelihood of retaining them as a valued team member.

I have sought to outline some of the challenges of achieving equitable pay amidst a global backdrop of financial crisis, teacher shortages and a gender pay gap in England, exemplified in a *Tes* headline reading 'Female teachers "work 81 days a year for free"' (Martin, 2023: 2).

We have explored the importance of stating your desired salary, point on the pay scale or remuneration package, supported with examples of why your request is appropriate. In addition, it's key to know your value and to disrupt inequity in salaries through considered preparation for a negotiation.

Disruptions

Three valuable disruptions that can be applied in practice include:

- Having your figure in mind prior to interview after doing careful research into what is equitable for you.
- Carefully considering what it may mean to proceed when you see a job advertisement inclusive of a 'competitive salary'. Be prepared and willing to explore what this may mean in real terms at interview.
- Making your qualifications pay you back by sharing a prepared outline of specific and relevant skills with your employer in an appropriate format (via interview/ in a negotiation meeting).

References

Academy of Management Insights (n.d.) *Debunking the 'women don't negotiate' pay-gap myth* [Online]. Available at: https://journals.aom.org/doi/10.5465/amd.2022.0021. summary (accessed 24 January 2024).

Choudry, S. (2019) 'Concrete ceilings and kinked hosepipes: Understanding the experiences of BME female leaders in schools', in V. Porritt and K. Featherstone (eds), *10% Braver: Inspiring Women to Lead Education*. London: SAGE Publications Ltd.

Half, R. (2023) 'How to negotiate salary after you get a job offer', *roberthalf*, 7 April [Online]. Available at: www.roberthalf.com/us/en/insights/career-development/be-ready-for-salary-negotiations-with-these-8-tips#toc6 (accessed 31 July 2023).

indeed (2023) 'How to negotiate a better salary', *uk.indeed*, 10 February [Online]. Available at: https://uk.indeed.com/career-advice/pay-salary/salary-negotiation (accessed 31 July 2023).

Lokenauth, A. [@FluentInFinance] (2023) 23 July [Twitter]. Available at: https://twitter.com/FluentInFinance/status/1682932964836147201?s=20 (accessed 31 July 2023).

Martin, M. (2023) 'Female teachers "work 81 days a year for free"', *Tes*, 23 February [Online]. Available at: www.tes.com/magazine/news/general/gender-pay-gap-education-teaching-women-work-free (accessed 31 July 2023).

Sibeta, L. (2023) 'What has happened to teacher pay in England?', *IFS*, 11 January [Online]. Available at: https://ifs.org.uk/articles/what-has-happened-teacher-pay-england (accessed 31 July 2023).

Tes (2023) 'Global teacher shortage: The rise in job vacancies', *Tes*, 17 March [Online]. Available at: www.tes.com/institute/blog/article/global-teacher-shortage-rise-job-vacancies (accessed 31 July 2023).

TesWorld (2020) 'Teacher interview technique: How do you negotiate pay in a teaching interview?', *YouTube*, 7 May [Online]. Available at: www.youtube.com/watch?app=desktop&v=RDAbs92ea2E (accessed 31 July 2023).

Whittaker, F. (2023) 'Keegan "keen" to look at varying teacher pay by subject, says union boss', *schoolsweek*, 18 January [Online]. Available at: https://schoolsweek.co.uk/keegan-keen-to-look-at-varying-teacher-pay-by-subject-says-union-boss/ (accessed 31 July 2023).

17

WHY ISN'T MY GENDER PAY GAP IMPROVING?

Sue Prickett

KEY POINTS

This chapter will:

- help leaders who don't think the gender pay gap is their responsibility
- advise anyone who wants to understand what the gender pay gap means
- share examples of strategies to reduce the gender pay gap
- explore how to disrupt and make specific change to practice within organisations.

Introduction

All schools have an operational team behind the scenes keeping the business running. In the UK, Multi-Academy Trusts (MAT) are groups of schools led by one business unit. My role within my MAT is Chief Finance and Operations Officer leading on finance and operations. As such, gender pay gap (GPG) reporting falls within my remit and I can influence strategy that should make our pay gap smaller with each year. I want to help everyone understand what the gender pay gap is. I'll also share a few simple ways of changing practice to disrupt the gender pay gap in the education sector in the UK and globally.

What the Heck Is a Gender Pay Gap Anyway?

Well, quite! Let me break it down and show how you can make a positive change to a global issue, simply by insisting on three specific practices: blind shortlisting; not asking for current salary information; and doing a simple maths calculation.

Gender pay gap for the uninitiated

The GPG is the difference in gross hourly earnings between women and men. It is based on salaries paid directly to employees before income tax and social security contributions are deducted. (EU Monitor, 2023)

Measuring the gap by the mean (average salary) and median (line the salaries up in ascending order and see which one is in the middle) removes some of the individual population demographic factors and allows organisations to compare pay for all roles on a level playing field.

A few facts

- 'Working women in the European Union (EU) earn on average 12.7% less per hour than men' (European Parliament, 2023).
- In the United Kingdom in 2023, 'Among all employees, the gender pay gap decreased to 14.9%' (ONS, 2023).

Breaking it down to the education sector, 'the analysis calculated using the latest Office for National Statistics (ONS) Annual survey of Hours and Earnings (ASHE) data, suggests that the gender pay gap for all staff working in any education organisation, including private companies, is 22.2%' (Martin, 2023). Please note this is not only schools.

Don't talk to me about percentages

So what does a GPG of 22.2% mean? In simple terms, for every £/$1 earnt by a male within the sector, a female earns 77.8 pence/cents – take 100 and minus 22.2. What does that sound like as a difference? Let's scale it up a bit and consider what it looks like using some indicative annual salaries from the 2023 UK Teaching and Support Staff salary ranges.

Table 17.1 Salaries based on 32.5 hrs/week, 52 weeks per annum

Pay Gap 22.2%	Male £1.00	Female £0.78p	Difference £0.22p
Classroom Assistant (term time only: 39 wks/pa)	£18,580	£14,455	£4,125
Early Career Teacher/Business Manager	£30,000	£23,340	£6,660
Later Career Teacher	£46,525	£36,196	£10,329
Middle Leader	£56,082	£43,632	£12,450
Senior Leader	£68,399	£53,214	£15,185
Executive Leader	£100,000	£77,800	£22,200

So if you are a middle leader, with a five point salary range made up of an increment of one point per year for five years in post, this could be a difference of over £60,000 during the five years. I can hear you all shouting, 'Surely this isn't true, because I can see the actual salary I am paid'. Yes, you can, but what about the salary everyone else is paid in your organisation, across the different roles? What if someone started in post after a career break due to caring responsibilities, accepted a lower salary because of it, and are a few years behind male counterparts?? Currently the UK employer contribution to the Teachers Pensions is 24.68%. If a middle leader loses out on actual salary payments of £60,000, that will have an impact of £14,808 on their pension contribution, not including interest and their own contributions. Sadly, if we consider there is also an ethnicity pay gap, 'Black and minoritised women see the compound effects of both the gender and ethnicity pay gaps' and 'compared to White British men, these pay gaps rise even further to 28.4%, 25.9%, and 25.0%, respectively' (Villie, 2024). The Fawcett Society (2023) also reports that the 'Motherhood Pay Penalty' – mothers with two children take home 26% less income than women without children – impacts on a woman's income and earning power throughout her working life, and compounds the effects of the ethnicity pay gap.

Let's consider days in a year

This will blow your mind.

Another very effective way of considering the pay gap is to calculate it in terms of Unpaid Days. Using the calculation of 365 days in a year, multiply that by the GPG of 22.2%, which gives us 81 days. So, from 1 January, women across the UK education sector work for free in comparison to their male colleagues for 81 days so they might as well not be paid until 21 March. Shocking, isn't it?

What Can I Do About it?

Challenge, communicate, and disrupt for change. Commit to educating everyone you know about the gender pay gap. Even if you don't know how to calculate it, you now know what it means. Also, we can all disrupt some of the practices that perpetuate the gender pay gap. Here are some important ways to disrupt.

Disruptions

Remove the question about previous salary from application forms and reference requests.

A simple way to contribute to reducing the GPG is to remove any reference to current or prior salary on an application form or at interview or a reference request. Why? Let me give you a real-life example.

An aspirational and gifted young teacher, newly qualified for a few years and steadily climbing the government set scale for teachers in England, dared to pause her career and have a baby. Whilst on maternity leave, she emailed to check whether she could apply for a post of middle leader with the answer, 'Of course, apply away'. She did, she got the job. No-one on the panel knew her current salary point. The interview panel read a well-prepared personal statement, experienced a positive interview, and watched gifted interactions with the student panel. The interview panel only knew the salary range of the job role they were appointing to. The candidate leapt years instead of steadily climbing one point after another. They smashed The Motherhood Penalty.

A point on a salary range does not equal competency. It may show several years in the sector, but it doesn't equal competency. Appoint to the job range you have advertised. Design your interview process so you do not need to rely on knowledge of previous salary for you to make an offer.

Blind shortlisting

Blind shortlisting means removing or redacting 'names, ages, personal pronouns, universities and qualifications' (Porritt et al., 2021).

Apart from removing unconscious bias for any protected characteristics, blind shortlisting and removing the previous salary box may also positively influence a gender pay gap. Perhaps a candidate wants to take a break and a step down from leadership, but still wants to stay in the sector. Perhaps they were made redundant in a previous post, a victim of bias where leadership didn't support and encourage progression. If one of the first boxes visible is their salary, how does that influence your decision to carry on reading the rest of the application? I cringed disclosing my own salary range of primary school business manager when applying for my next step up as a leader and Chief Financial Officer of a trust. It was one of the first boxes on the paper application form. They would have had to read much further to find out about my relevant qualifications and a career break to raise my three children. Imagine if they had discarded me because I wasn't earning enough to be any good. An interesting example is how orchestras began using blind auditions with musicians playing behind screens:

> ... researchers have determined that this step alone makes it 50% more likely that a woman will advance to the finals. And the screen has also been demonstrated to be the source of a surge in the number of women being offered positions. (Rice, 2013)

Challenge practice – know your own context

One of the biggest challenges is convincing those in leadership of the need to change. If you sit on interview panels regularly, look out for your own examples such as the ones I've given. Call out those who discard an application because someone has the wrong salary in the box. Talk to your leaders, including governance, and take time to help them understand what the gap means. Read around the topic, it's surprisingly interesting once you start, though check your blood pressure regularly!

Chief Financial Officers (CFOs) and Human Resource (HR) leaders do your salary audits. Are people with similar responsibilities paid the same? Compare support staff responsibilities to teaching responsibilities and check the salaries. Is your Business Manager earning less than your other middle or senior leaders, whilst accepting an equal level but different type of responsibility? Look outside of the education sector to benchmark job roles. Don't fear the GPG calculation. If you have access to a maths class of teenagers, give them the anonymised data set and get them to do it for you.

Challenge responsibly with fact and metrics

We are in an era of information and data overload. So many software platforms produce metric dashboards of staff gender split these days. Use these metrics to drive the change. Check the gender split of applicants and target your recruitment strategy. Change the language to attract more male early career teachers and support staff into your schools.

> Research by the recruitment website TotalJobs 2017 analysed more than 75,000 job adverts over a six-week period and found an average of six stereotypically 'male' and 'female' words in each advert. (Tickle, 2018)

Children need those male role models. They also need to see effective and transformative female leaders. Consider the language in the adverts for Heads of Schools, Principals, Business and Operations Managers and ensure it isn't overly masculinised.

Challenge outside our own organisation: Suppliers beware!

Having worked hard within my own organisation to remove the salary box from our paper application forms, we moved to an electronic applicant tracking system a few years ago. I had the opportunity to discuss the impact of the salary box with the founder and CEO of a teacher recruitment platform. I explained we didn't use it on our application forms and gave him a potted version of this chapter. It was the first time he'd heard of the impact salary boxes can have on the gender pay gap. He went away, learnt more about it, surveyed his client base, and came up with the option to toggle off the salary box. My next challenge to him will be to have the default setting as off and for schools to have to switch it on (if they must). Perhaps we should introduce a flash warning and sirens that this action could be detrimental to the GPG in education! We also use budgeting software that has developed a report showing whether my GPG is improving in future years as I input my assumptions. This very simple report lets me instantly know the effect of appointing male or female to a vacancy in future years which is impressive. Does your budgeting software do this?

Challenge yourself – be the change, be the disrupter!

If you are in a position of leadership, either in education management or business operations of educational organisations, you can make the changes happen by simply having the conversations.

If you are not in leadership, it doesn't stop you planting the seed with those who are. Start the ball rolling today and change the future for the women of tomorrow.

References

EU Monitor (2023) *Understanding the gender pay gap* [Online]. Available at: www. eumonitor.eu/9353000/1/j9vvik7m1c3gyxp/vl59mpupm0vq?ctx=vk4jic6t1dxz (accessed 23 January 2024).

European Parliament (2023) *Understanding the gender pay gap* [Online]. Available at: www. eumonitor.eu/9353000/1/j9vvik7m1c3gyxp/vl59mpupm0vq?ctx=vk4jic6t1dxz (accessed 23 January 2024).

Martin, M. (2023) 'Female teachers "work 81 days a year for free"', *Tes*, 23 February [Online]. Available at: www.tes.com/magazine/news/general/gender-pay-gap-education-teaching-women-work-free (accessed 23 January 2024).

Office of National Statistics [ONS] (2023) *Gender pay gap in the UK* [Online]. Available at: www.ons.gov.uk/employmentandlabourmarket/peopleinwork/earningsandworkinghours/bulletins/genderpaygapintheuk/2023 (accessed 23 January 2024).

Porritt, V., Hannay, L. and Plummer, P. (2021) 'Deliberate disruption: Issues of gender and diversity', *Impact*, 11 [Online]. Available at: https://my.chartered.college/impact_article/deliberate-disruption-issues-of-gender-and-diversity/ (accessed 20 January 2024).

Rice, C. (2013) 'How blind auditions help orchestras to eliminate gender bias', *The Guardian*, 14 October [Online]. Available at: www.theguardian.com/women-in-leadership/2013/oct/14/blind-auditions-orchestras-gender-bias (accessed 20 January 2024).

The Fawcett Society (2023) *Fawcett research shows black and minoritised mothers hit hardest by pay penalty* [Online]. Available at: www.fawcettsociety.org.uk/News/ethnicity-motherhood-pay-penalty (accessed 23 January 2024).

Tickle, L. (2018) 'Language in school job ads puts women off headteacher roles', *The Guardian*, 19 June [Online]. Available at: www.theguardian.com/education/2018/jun/19/language-school-headteacher-job-ads-puts-women-off (accessed 23 January 2024).

Villie, L. (2024) *Double trouble: The ethnicity Gender Pay Gap* [Online]. Available at: www. fawcettsociety.org.uk/Handlers/Download.ashx?IDMF=db2a690e-c6b2-4c9d-b9ea-39e36cdc7e70 (accessed 25 January 2024).

18

MIND THE GAP? YES, SO LET'S DO SOMETHING ABOUT IT!

Abigail Mann

KEY POINTS

This chapter will:

- explore the relationship between the patriarchy and the gender pay gap
- examine the gender pay gap in education
- examine the role of both men and women in addressing the gender pay gap.

Introduction

This chapter is about understanding the gender pay gap, knowing your worth, and calling upon men and women to do something about it. It includes knowledge, a case study, and advice to empower you to know your worth.

If you're reading this, I'd bet my entire Charles Dickens collection that you already know what the gender pay gap is, but in the interests of clarity here's a summary. The Office for National Statistics (ONS) states the gender pay gap is 'the difference between average hourly earnings (excluding overtime) of men and women as a proportion of men's average hourly earnings (excluding overtime)' (ONS, 2022).

Patriarchy and the Gender Pay Gap

To understand the issues facing women, it's important to uncover its possible origins – or at least, one of the reasons it exists: the patriarchy.

Patriarchy is a social construct that has not been around since the emergence of humans. Indeed, for most of our existence, women have not been seen as subordinate to men. Its origins are traced back to Mesopotamia, a time when the lifestyle experience of humans changed from roaming societies to that of static agricultural communities. Before this, societies worldwide were matrilineal; they were structured around, and kinship was traced through, the mother. Evidence exists all over Europe of peaceful, prosperous societies led by women for thousands of years (Gerlich, 2018).

As Western societies evolved, patriarchy emerged. In its earliest form it was seen as a way for men to gain power and control not just over women, but in society at large.

Thousands of years later, and despite societal structural change including historical changes like suffrage and more contemporary social movements like the United Nations #HeforShe campaign (2023), the impact of patriarchy is still seen.

Put simply, since the emergence of patriarchy and the archaic view that women are seen as subordinate to men, some women have had to fight for their worth and for their voices to be heard. Not only has it negatively impacted upon some male leaders' views of women, subconsciously or not, but it has adversely affected how some women view themselves and their own self-worth. If you haven't felt the pangs of imposter syndrome at any time in your professional life, you're doing better than I am. So, where do we go from here? It's important to explore the UK gender pay gap as it currently stands.

The UK gender pay gap

The current overall gap in the UK is 14.9% (TUC, 2023). This is calculated by using all median hourly pay for male and female employees with data taken from the Office for National Statistics (ONS) Annual Survey of Hours and Earnings. When turned into days, this means that women, on average, currently work 54 days per year for free. For free!

How does this compare to the gender pay gap in education?

The gender pay gap in education

The gap in education is worse. It currently sits at 22.2%, equating to 81 days of free work by women per year (TUC, 2023). Note that this data is for the entire education sector, which includes not only schools but colleges, higher education institutions and private education companies. Senior leadership positions continue to be overrepresented by men in both primary and secondary schools despite the education profession being predominantly female. In a report on trends in education it was reported:

> In primary schools in 2020, female teachers made up 85% of the workforce compared with 74% of headteachers; in secondary schools, female teachers made up 63% of the workforce compared with 40% of headteachers. (DfE, 2022)

At classroom teacher level, women earn 2.4% less than males in the same role. At leadership level, women earn 11.3% less than male Headteachers. This difference widens with age and seniority of position, and in 2022, the difference by age 60 and over for heads reached an average £15,961 (ASCL et al., 2023). The gender pay gap is alive in education.

So what can we do? Knowing your worth means accepting the gap exists, equipping yourself with the knowledge to disrupt the status quo and do something about it. The following case study involves all those things.

If You Don't Ask, You'll Never Know

This case study is my own to share. What follows is a story of a chance question that revealed a gender pay discrepancy.

It begins at the end. The outcome is positive. It involves a backdated payment, a raise in salary and a promotion. None of these things would have materialised, however, if I hadn't had the courage to ask a simple but bold question.

The question? Can you help to finance my Master's degree?

I asked this question to the Headteacher of a previous school in which I worked. The answer was simple enough. No. What followed was a well-meaning confessional of sorts which led to the discovery that I was being paid less than my male counterparts in like-for-like roles. The Headteacher explained that for some time I had been paid less than the department leads for Maths and Science, both males, and that they would like to rectify the situation by paying me the same. This would go some way to supporting the financing of my degree, they explained.

I was completely shocked. I had successfully led a high-performing English department in the school for two years. Both of my male counterparts had not achieved the same outcomes, and both had begun their employment there after my own. What I discovered felt unfair and indeed illegal according to the Equality Act 2010.

I sought advice from my union who were quick to confirm that the difference in pay was neither fair nor correct and that I was within my rights to ask that the discrepancy be corrected. It was important to me at this stage that the next steps were considered carefully. Up to this point, I'd had a trusting, respectful relationship with the Headteacher, and I did not wish for this to change. I arranged a meeting to discuss things.

At the meeting, which I attended unrepresented, I set out my concerns with what had occurred. One of the male members of staff had been paid more than me for over a year, whilst the other had only four months of additional pay due to their respective starting points. I sought recompense. The headteacher went on to explain that the reason for the discrepancy in pay had been about teacher recruitment and shortage subjects requiring greater incentives to take up roles. Whilst I understood this perspective and couldn't begin to imagine the difficult decisions Headteachers have to make to ensure classrooms have teachers, it still didn't seem fair that I had been paid differently for such a significant amount of time. The Head offered to backdate the pay from September of the current academic year. I explained that this didn't seem fair either and we both left the meeting to think over next steps.

After seeking further advice from my union representative, I again addressed the issue with the Headteacher and, with a supporting letter from my union, the Headteacher agreed to backdate the pay from the time the discrepancy arose. I was happy with the result and felt I had handled the situation with due care, but worried about the relationship I had with the Headteacher. I need not have. The relationship was sustained and, although tested through a difficult issue, remained intact. The following month I applied for an Associate Assistant Headteacher role and was thrilled when I was offered the position.

Whilst this anecdote ends positively, I am mindful that the same can't be said for many other women who may have found themselves in similar positions. When I reflected on this event, I thought about some of the reasons it concluded in a fair and respectful way. Knowing my worth was at the forefront of all decisions made. It instilled confidence in my decision-making because I knew the cause was important and I felt supported by the law.

I now want to ensure that leaders of educational organisations work through the issues that will enable them to ensure equitable treatment for women in the workplace.

Disruptions

The role of male leaders

By taking these actions, you are both supporting your female colleagues in achieving equal pay and positively disrupting the current inequalities surrounding the topic.

Clarity: know the legalities of employment law and ensure they are followed. Decision-making, balancing the needs of all stakeholders, and getting the right teachers in front of students is no easy feat. You cannot and will not please everyone, but you can and must operate within the legal framework, including that of equal pay for the same or equivalent role. As male leaders, you have a responsibility to ensure that equal pay is adhered to for your female colleagues. You must:

- be open and transparent about pay in your organisation
- ensure both men and women are paid fairly at all levels
- champion equal pay in your Headteacher networks and share your commitment to it.

The role of male professionals

Challenge and collaboration: support female colleagues and challenge the status quo.

Female educators cannot fight this battle alone. We need our male colleagues to join the debate and proactively engage in change for the better. One way in which this can be done is when joining an organisation, ask about gender pay:

- be bold – directly ask your potential employer whether females who are currently in like-for-like roles are paid the same salary as you are being offered

- look up the gender pay gap of the organisation where you work and directly ask the employer about equality and the gender pay gap for all roles in their organisation (https://gender-pay-gap.service.gov.uk/viewing/search-results?t=1&search=E-Act&orderBy=relevance).

Another way in which male colleagues can support is by spreading the word. We need your voices too! Talk to colleagues about gender and pay:

- talk about it in the staff room
- spread the word on social media sites like X (formerly Twitter) and LinkedIn
- mention it at conferences in your presentation or during networking.

The more the issue is openly discussed, the more likely it is that leaders will hear the message and address change in their organisations. Shout it from the rooftops: change must happen.

The role of female professionals

Confidence: use your voice and don't be afraid to ask for what you deserve.

It could have been easy for me to take the first answer my previous employer had given me. Difficult conversations are never straightforward, but it wouldn't have been the right thing to do. So, however uncomfortable you may feel, having conversations around pay is imperative.

Expect absolute clarity and equality. Ask about gender and pay. The Equality Act (2010) states it's unlawful to stop employees from disclosing a difference in salary if they're trying to ascertain whether an equal pay issue between male and female employees exists.

Speak up and the gender pay gap is challenged. Stay silent and it isn't.

References

ASCL, NAHT, nga and WomenEd (2023) *Gender pay gap for secondary heads widest for a decade, warn education organisations* [Online]. Available at: https://www.ascl.org.uk/News/Our-news-and-press-releases/Gender-pay-gap-for-secondary-heads-widest-for-a-de (accessed 20 January 2024).

Department for Education (DfE) (2022) *School leadership in England 2010 to 2020: Characteristics and trends* [Online]. Available at: https://assets.publishing.service.gov.uk/government/uploads/system/uploads/attachment_data/file/1071794/School_leadership_in_England_2010_to_2020_characteristics_and_trends_-_report.pdf (accessed 20 January 2024).

Gerlich, R. (2018) *The creation of patriarchy: How did it happen?* [Online]. Available at: https://reneejg.net/2018/12/creation-of-patriarchy/ (accessed 20 January 2024).

Office for National Statistics (2022) *Gender pay gap in the UK: 2022. Differences in pay between women and men by age, region, full-time and part-time, and occupation* [Online]. Available at: www.ons.gov.uk/employmentandlabourmarket/peopleinwork/earningsandworkinghours/bulletins/genderpaygapintheuk/2022 (accessed 20 January 2024).

TUC Press Office (2023) *Gender Pay Gap means women work for free for two months of the year* [Online]. Available at: www.tuc.org.uk/news/gender-pay-gap-means-women-work-free-two-months-year-tuc (accessed 20 January 2024).

CASE STUDY 4

THE GENDER PAY GAP IN A HIGHER EDUCATION ORGANISATION

Stephani Dupree

Lena sat at her desk, staring at the email that had just popped up in her inbox. She couldn't believe what she was reading. It was her performance review, and even though she had worked tirelessly for the past year, her boss had given her a less than satisfactory rating. She knew it was because she was a woman. Lena had heard whispers about the gender pay gap at her company, but she never thought it would affect her.

As she sat there, her mind raced with questions. Was it fair that she was being paid less than her male colleagues? How could she close the pay gap? What could she do to ensure that women at her organisation were treated fairly and given the same opportunities as men?

Lena knew that she wasn't alone in this struggle. The gender pay gap was a problem that affected millions of women across the country. Despite the progress that had been made in recent years, women were still earning less than men for the same work. It was a systemic issue that needed to be addressed.

Determined to do something about it, Lena started to do her research. She read articles and studies about the gender pay gap, and she talked to other women in her industry who had experienced the same discrimination. She learned that the pay gap was not just a result of women being paid less for the same work, but also because women were often in lower-paying jobs and were less likely to be promoted to higher-paying positions.

Lena knew that it was time for her to disrupt. She scheduled a meeting with her boss to discuss her performance review and the gender pay gap at their company. She came armed with facts and figures and made a compelling argument for why women deserved to be paid the same as men. To her surprise, her boss listened and agreed to work with her to close the gap.

From that moment on, Lena became a vocal advocate for gender equality in the workplace. She worked with other women at her organisation to form a diversity and inclusion committee, and they started to implement policies and programmes that would help to close the pay gap. It wasn't easy, but they persevered, and over time, they saw real progress.

Lena's journey is just one example of the many women who are fighting for equality in the workplace. The gender pay gap is a problem that won't be solved overnight, but with dedication and perseverance, we can make real progress. It's time for women to be 10% braver and stand up and demand the same opportunities and pay as their male colleagues.

CASE STUDY 5

DISRUPT THE GENDER PAY GAP

KNOW YOUR WORTH

Jess Gosling

As an international teacher, I have been part of a system that often does not provide pay scales or clarity on salaries. Some schools do, which I find highly appealing and a more just approach, but these are still few and far between.

This of course can be quite frustrating, but as my male partner and I both teach, when offered renumeration details I am able to see schools that are willing to treat us both equally, or those who place me on a different starting point due to my maternity leave.

My maternity leave from full-time education was five years in length, but I expect to be placed on the same salary starting point as my partner as we both qualified as teachers in the same year. This has been so far successful. If it were not, my argument would be whilst raising my child, I studied for a Master's in Early Years, set up my own early years business and continued to teach, albeit part-time. In addition, the most effective professional development I have received was supporting my own child's development from 0–4 years.

More recently, I have had the courage to negotiate a higher starting salary for both of us. In international schools, this is possible. I first learnt of this in a discussion with my colleagues. They explained they negotiated their salary in every teaching role. It is nerve-wracking perhaps to think about doing this, but why not try?

Through working so hard to ensure I am the best teacher I can be, I gain the confidence to request better pay or benefits. I did just this: citing my wealth of experience in my field and what I was able to bring to the school, especially in terms of training others in supporting English as an Additional Language learners.

Know your worth and be bold and, of course, 10% braver.

PART IV
FLEXIBLE WORKING
CULTURE CHANGE REQUIRED

INTRODUCTION
Vivienne Porritt

This section includes discussion of working part-time, as you would expect. It is also about the myriad other ways that the education section needs a complete culture change regarding flexible working, thinking and leadership. To me, the concepts that come to mind when building an organisational culture include:

- vision and strategy
- innovation and integrity
- trust and achievement.

The authors in this section highlight the lack of several of these concepts in the way some leaders treat women, in particular, who want to educate and lead and be a parent. Other corporate sectors are getting a better handle on this balancing act:

> The provision of flexible working can help firms attract and retain a wider range of workers, including parents, people with caring responsibilities, younger and older workers and those with a disability or a health condition. Flexible working may also amount to a reasonable adjustment under the Equality Act 2010. (CIPD, 2023: paragraph 3)

I appreciate concerns about timetable and locations. However, innovative and flexible leaders can and do make flex happen as seen in the case studies curated by WomenEd and partners (Chartered College of Teaching, n.d.) and the case studies and ideas shared across this section. What I learned is the importance of treating educators and leaders as human beings, and respecting their needs and hopes. If we can't do that in education, we contribute to the global recruitment crisis as highlighted across this section. Heed the advice given on how to treat women experiencing the menopause or tragic loss; they want to contribute as and when they can, so please, afford them this dignity.

As our authors show, there are multiple ways to make flex work across our workplaces and there are many options available for women whose organisations say flex is not possible. I love Lindsay Patience's reminder that flex can be a request to drop a child off once a week or attend a staff meeting remotely. The crux is talking with and listening to your colleagues with an intent to find a way forward. As Kerry Jordan-Daus and Wendy Cobb ask, 'What's your problem with flexible working?'.

(See: https://womened.com/flexible-working-campaign)

References

Chartered College of Teaching (n.d.) *Flexible working* [Online]. Available at: https://chartered.college/flexible-working/ (accessed 27 January 2024).

CIPD (2023) *Flexible working: The business case* [Online]. Available at: www.cipd.org/globalassets/media/knowledge/knowledge-hub/reports/2023-pdfs/2023-flexible-working-the-business-case-august.pdf (accessed 27 January 2024).

19

FLEXIBLE WORKING

A SUSTAINABLE SOLUTION?

Ruth Astley

KEY POINTS

This chapter will:

- explore the need for organisational changes to make flexible working a sustainable choice
- provide a personal narrative of being a woman, a senior leader and a mother working part-time
- show how I began influencing attitudes to drive change by giving women leaders a voice
- outline the changes I implemented to connect, support, and empower current and future women leaders.

Introduction

> It may not be enough simply to make part-time work available. In order to truly make a difference in the quality of life for women with children, part-time work must also be made desirable and rewarding. (Higgins et al., 2000: 29)

This quotation resonated deeply, reflecting my own experience of working part-time since 2014. In 2019, the Department for Education (DfE, 2019) began encouraging and promoting the benefits of flexible working in education. Yet while numbers of teachers working part-time have increased over this time period, women aged 30–39 show the highest increase in attrition rates in schools (DfE, 2023). This chapter will explore organisational changes that needed to happen in my own school to ensure the sustainability of flexible working.

Background

Women are having children later than ever, leading to greater conflicts within already established careers (Young, 2018). Increasing use of terms such as 'concrete ceiling', 'sticky floors' and 'leaky pipelines' reflects the limits placed on women's careers, the lack of leadership advancement opportunities and the restriction of women to the lower rungs of organisations. These limits restrict gender diversity and exacerbate the gender pay gap (Ciminelli et al., 2021).

Jonathon Simons proposed that greater use of flexible working for teachers was the solution to the 'huge bulge in leavers for women aged between 30–39' (2016: 17). Since 2017, government-driven initiatives have sought to increase the uptake of flexible working (DfE, 2017; Foster, 2018) and to support the recruitment, retention and motivation of teachers, improve wellbeing and improve the gender pay gap by retaining women within the profession, encouraging their careers to progress (DfE, 2017, 2021).

School workforce statistics (DfE, 2023) would suggest these initiatives are working, with an increase in the percentage of teachers working part-time from 21.4% in 2010 to 24.2% by 2021, and higher and increasing proportions of those working part-time being women (25.6% in 2010 increasing to 29% by 2022/23).

If flexible working is an important disruption to gender inequality and if the numbers have been increasing, why am I still asking a question about its sustainability?

This is where things become a little more personal.

Being a Woman, a Senior Leader, a Mother and Working Part-Time

I was a secondary school Advanced Skills Teacher in 2013 when I had my first child and began working three days a week. I had started a part-time Master of Education degree, which I finished when my daughter was two, writing through her lunchtime nap. Working part-time allowed me to continue in my professional role, spend time with my daughter and *challenge* myself through study.

Over the following four years I had two more children, establishing a good balance between home and work, with clear boundaries; it was demanding but rewarding. However, while colleagues progressed their careers, I missed an opportunity for promotion because it was not shared with me while on maternity leave. It seemed career advancement was something I would have to wait for.

By September 2020, things shifted. As a Lead Practitioner I had been responsible for our Pupil Premium strategy, but the profile and scope of this role had expanded significantly because of the pandemic. I was invited to join the Senior Leadership Team (SLT) to drive the whole-school approach to supporting our disadvantaged students.

Suddenly, lines between home and work blurred. Before the pandemic, my non-working days involved activities with my children, keeping my boundaries in place. I was now home during an uncertain and anxious time, checking work emails or attending SLT Zoom meetings on my non-working day, my kids subdued with snacks and TV in the background.

Over the next three years I had to work much harder to claw back that balance and got it very wrong at times. I asked myself whether progressing my leadership career while working part-time was possible, let alone sustainable. I felt it should be.

Navigating and balancing my intersecting roles as a woman, a senior leader and a mother of three, working part-time in a secondary school, I felt responsibility as a role model, to support the career development and retention of others. My study for a second Master's degree in Education Leadership and Management provided the perfect platform to explore this.

It's not just me

I looked at what had already been published, and found I was not the only one struggling. By 2022, women aged 30–39 showed the highest increase in attrition rates (DfE, 2023), and the 2021/22–2022/23 school workforce data show the first decrease in those working part-time in over a decade to 23.9%.

The Department for Education (2019) acknowledged a gap in literature drawing on the direct experiences of those working part-time. Fortunately, a slowly increasing number of publications and organisations joined WomenEd (Featherstone and Porritt, 2021) in exploring these voices: Zoe Young (2018), Emma Turner (2020); Flex Teacher Talent, Lindsay Patience and Lucy Rose (2022); Anna Whitehouse (2023); *Pregnant then Screwed*, Joeli Brearley (2023); and the Maternity Teacher/Paternity Teacher (MTPT) project, Emma Sheppard (2023). Their words gave me the *confidence* to pursue this work.

Listening to Others

To drive *change* within my own school, I recognised that it was more powerful not to rely solely on my own experiences but to listen to other women leaders who were mothers working part-time. Bringing them together, though logistically challenging, allowed all to communicate their thoughts. I offered a series of prompts and let the conversation flow in a series of powerful focus groups and interviews. They valued the chance to talk about their experience, build a *connection* with each other, and find they were not alone but part of a *community*.

Influencing Attitudes

I wanted to *challenge* and disrupt the current position. The protected characteristics of Sex, Pregnancy and Maternity made it appropriate to present this work within a Diversity,

Equity, and Inclusion Framework. Adopting Booth and Ainscow's (2002) three dimensions of Culture, Policies and Practices for inclusion to frame the women's voices I could show that these were needed to underpin flexible working and enable it to become a sustainable choice. Flexible working on its own was not enough of a solution.

Figure 19.1 shows the themes identified in the women's experiences, all of which I recognised. Without deliberate organisational change conducted in *collaboration* with those affected to address these three dimensions, they were at risk of leaving the profession. Sharing the voices of my colleagues meant it was no longer my lone voice asking for change; the collective demand was much more influential.

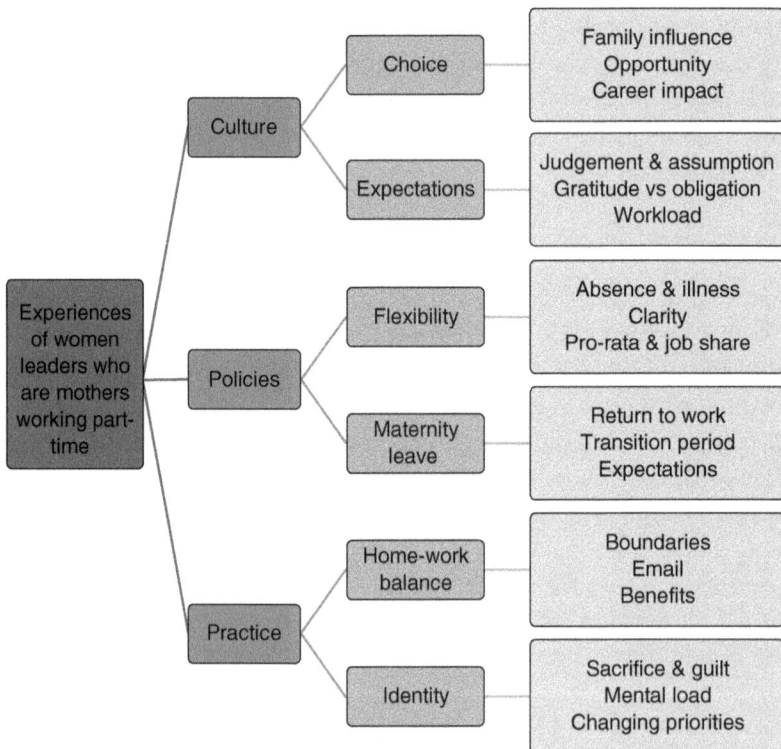

Figure 19.1 Women's experiences: Network analysis showing the identified themes (adapted from Thomas, 2013: 238)

Organisational Change

Creating inclusive cultures

As a result of sharing the experiences of my colleagues, I received approval to develop a family-friendly strategy. The first step was to create a centralised website for sharing all things family friendly, particularly around flexible working and maternity, to ensure clarity and consistency.

Where these women have been offered choice and opportunity in their career path, they have felt positive: 'I do feel this has created a feeling of loyalty … and, in turn, has led to a purposeful and driven approach to my career' (Reid, personal communication, 20 December 2022).

To ensure that teachers working part-time or on maternity leave feel that opportunities for career progression are not only available but actively encouraged, our job adverts state that we are open to flexible working and are shared directly with those on maternity leave.

Developing inclusive policies

The women I interviewed found the period of pregnancy, maternity leave and returning to work anxious and stressful. Reviewing our policies through the lens of these teachers drove change.

Relevant policies are now shared on the staff site so there is no need for these to be requested, ensuring ease of access to all. A guidance handbook, alongside statutory policies on maternity and flexible working provides additional clarity and consistency about expectations and entitlements, around both maternity (such as the use of keeping-in-touch (KIT) days) and flexible working (for example, payment for attendance on non-working days). Striving to be as inclusive as possible, this also includes shared parental leave, paternity leave, adoption and surrogacy leave and our menopause policy.

Evolving inclusive practices

The women valued making connections: 'How enlightening to hear other people saying the things you thought you felt in isolation. It has been such a powerful experience to spend time with other people navigating the pressures of sustaining a career whilst balancing a family' (Reid, personal communication, 20 December 2022).

Impact

Colleagues have been enthusiastic about what we have done: 'This is BRILLIANT. Clear and easy to navigate – I wish this had been in play when I came back the first time' (Watson, personal communication, 18 July 2023). Others have approached me to discuss various aspects in more detail, and I see a positive impact within my organisation through increasing numbers working part-time, including leaders, male teachers, and women without children, showing that the benefits of flexible working are not confined to women with young children.

As someone who envisages always wanting some element of flexible working in my career, I will always push for a family-friendly approach. Through addressing the culture, policies and practices within my organisation, I am confident I can help to make flexible working a sustainable solution for our staff. I hope that by sharing this work, it can support others to drive similar changes in their own schools.

Disruptions

- Listen to the voices of those working flexibly. All schools are different – what are their experiences?
- Reflect on the culture, policies and practices from the perspective of those working flexibly and make changes. See the organisation through their lens.
- Share the message that making flexible working sustainable benefits everyone, not just women and not just mothers.
- Create opportunities to connect flexible working women leaders together.

References

Booth, T. and Ainscow, M. (2002) *Index for inclusion: Developing learning and participation in schools* [Online]. Available at: www.eenet.org.uk/resources/docs/Index%20English.pdf (accessed 30 October 2023).

Brearley, J. (2023) *About pregnant then screwed* [Online]. Available at: https://pregnantthenscrewed.com/about-maternity-discrimination/ (accessed 30 October 2023).

Ciminelli, G., Schwellnus, C. and Stadler, B. (2021) *Sticky floors or glass ceilings? The role of human capital, working time flexibility and discrimination in the gender wage gap*, OECD Economics Department Working Papers 1668 [Online]. Available at: www.oecd-ilibrary.org/docserver/02ef3235-en.pdf (accessed 30 October 2023)

Department for Education (2017) *New support for flexible working in schools pledged at summit, UK* [Online]. Available at: www.gov.uk/government/news/new-support-for-flexible-working-in-schools-pledged-at-summit (accessed 30 October 2023).

Department for Education (2019) *Benefits of flexible working for teachers and schools, UK* [Online]. Available at: www.gov.uk/government/publications/benefits-of-flexible-working-for-teachers-and-schools (accessed 30 October 2023).

Department for Education (2021) *Flexible working ambassador schools* [Online]. Available at: www.gov.uk/guidance/flexible-working-ambassador-schools#overview (accessed 30 October 2023).

Department for Education (2023) *School workforce in England* [Online]. Available at: https://explore-education-statistics.service.gov.uk/data-tables/permalink/1f1059b4-bbba-4a93-935a-08db6e4a05c2 (accessed 30 October 2023).

Featherstone, K. and Porritt, V. (2021) *Being 10% Braver*. London: Sage.

Foster, D. (2018) *Teacher Recruitment and Retention in England*. Briefing Paper Number 7222. London: House of Commons Library [Online]. Available at: https://dera.ioe.ac.uk/32668/1/CBP-7222%20%281%29.pdf (accessed 30 October 2023).

Higgins, C., Duxbury, L. and Johnson, K. (2000) 'Part-time work for women: Does it really help balance work and family?', *Human Resource Management*, 39(1), 17–32.

Patience, L. and Rose, L. (2022) *Flex Education: A Guide for Flexible Working in Schools*. London: Sage.

Sheppard, E. (2023) *A Guide to Teaching, Parenting and Creating Family Friendly Schools: The MaternityTeacher PaternityTeacher Project Handbook*. Oxon: Routledge.

Simons, J. (2016) *The importance of teachers: A collection of essays on teacher recruitment and retention* [Online]. Available at: https://policyexchange.org.uk/wp-content/uploads/2016/03/the-Importance-of-Teachers.pdf (accessed 30 October 2023).

Thomas, G. (2013) *How to do your Research Project: A Guide for Students in Education and Applied Social Sciences*, 2nd edn. London: Sage.

Turner, E. (2020) *Let's Talk About Flex: Flipping the Flexible Working Narrative for Education.* Woodbridge: John Catt.

Whitehouse, A. (2023) *Flex appeal* [Online]. Available at: www.motherpukka.co.uk/flex/ (accessed 30 October 2023).

Young, Z. (2018) *Women's Work: How Mothers Manage Flexible Working in Careers and Family Life.* Bristol: Bristol University Press.

20

THE FUTURE OF FLEXIBLE WORKING – THE IMPACT OF THE EMPLOYMENT RELATIONS (FLEXIBLE WORKING) ACT

Lindsay Patience

KEY POINTS

This chapter will:

- discuss new legislation on flexible working which will impact all UK employers, including schools
- highlight that schools with a reactive approach to flexible working will likely feel the impact of these changes more
- argue that school leaders globally should be considering flexible working as an opportunity to address the global recruitment crisis rather than because of changes in the law.

Introduction

In 2024, significant legal changes for flexible working have been introduced in the UK due to the Employment Relations (Flexible Working) Act 2023. The Government have taken heed of pressure from many different groups campaigning for better flexible working opportunities. This new legislation came about following a consultation centred around making flexible working the default position for employers. The education sector often lags behind other sectors when it comes to Human Resources (HR), and personnel matters and many school leaders will worry about how these new guidelines and rules will affect them. I advocate the option to embrace these changes and capitalise on the opportunities they can bring.

The Main Legal Changes

The key changes are that:

- employees can request flexible working from their first day of employment rather than waiting until they have been employed for 26 weeks
- employees are no longer limited to one statutory request per year, they can make two in a 12-month period
- employers must respond to flexible working requests within two months rather than three as previously.

A Change in Approach

There is still a guiding principle that it 'remains a right to request, not a right to have flexible working' (Department for Business, Energy & Industrial Strategy, 2021). So, schools are still not under any obligation to agree to flexible working requests, they need only consider the requests in a reasonable manner. However, there is a definite move towards treating requests seriously and more positively. If requests are met with an approach of wanting to make this work, rather than dismissing it as too hard, then more requests will be approved and what is requested is more likely to suit the needs of the school.

There is a new focus on communicating about the request and the details of how the flex might work. Employers are encouraged to have meaningful conversations with those requesting flexible working and work together to look at different options before the formal decision is made. It used to be the case that employees had to set out in detail in their request how the effects of their flexible working request might impact and be dealt with by their employer. This never sat well with me because the requestor rarely has the full picture of how their flexibility might affect others, but more importantly, often when people are requesting flexible working, it is because of a difficult time or changing circumstances such as a new baby, a health issue, or the need to care for a family member. People may well be vulnerable in these times and having to focus energy into detailing the potential impact of your flexible working request can be gruelling and time consuming. It is emotionally charged and might be difficult due to personal circumstances. At Flexible Teacher Talent, we support teachers and leaders with their flexible working applications, and many feel like they are wasting their time and they will be met with an inevitable rejection. It's not easy to muster the strength for such a task when you have a newborn or a health concern yourself or for a loved one.

Impact on Employers and Employees

Possible impacts of the new legislation on those approving flexible working requests include:

- more requests to deal with
- more time to consider requests
- need to respond more quickly
- need for discussion of the decision with applicant and opportunity to consider alternatives
- requests for flexibility at job offer stage.

Possible impacts of the new legislation on those making flexible working requests include:

- can try to negotiate flexibility at any time from the job offer stage
- can make a further request if the initial one is turned down
- reduced requirement to explain impact of the flexible working request on the school
- more opportunity to discuss and negotiate the proposed arrangements and consider alternatives.

How This May Impact Schools and Trusts

In practice, for school leaders and those applying for flexible working, how much impact these legislative changes will make to the day-to-day running of the school and people's lives is yet to be seen. It might be that some schools continue to think flexible working is too difficult for them and still refuse to engage with it. Not only will these schools be missing out on all of the opportunities that flexible working can bring (for retention, recruitment, staff wellbeing, diversity, productivity), they may also find themselves facing an increased administrative burden associated with the flexible working requests they are turning down. More employees can make requests and they can make them more often, and the employer will have to engage in the decision-making process more. They will have to discuss the request with the employee and the reason for rejecting it and consider alternatives and compromises, and they will have to do this in a shorter time than previously. So, schools may find themselves devoting more time to considering flexible working requests, particularly if the trend for increased demand for flexibility continues.

However, some schools might already do much of what the new legislation requires and so the changes will have very little impact on them. Antonia Spinks, CEO of the Pioneer Education Trust, talks about how, in their schools, they have a clear system in place for colleagues to request flexible working and, wherever possible, these are agreed to. They already deal with flexible working requests in the way that the new legal guidance outlines. 'Flexible working arrangements in place, wherever possible' is one of the pillars of their WorkWell Strategy for staff (Pioneer Educational Trust, n.d). Antonia talks about their culture in treating colleagues as professional adults who are encouraged to make positive choices in identifying how to manage their workload, achieve work–life balance and nurture their own wellbeing. As one of the Department for Education's Flexible Working Ambassador Multi-Academy Trusts and Schools in England (Department for Education, 2023), Pioneer supports other trust and school leaders with introducing and managing flexible working for their staff too. Antonia is a compelling advocate for the benefits of flexible working in schools. She, and others like her, have not waited for changes in the law before making flexible working work 'wherever possible'.

A Proactive vs Reactive Approach

My organisation, Flexible Teacher Talent, has long advocated for schools to take a proactive approach to flexible working, and the previous paragraph illustrates why schools continuing with a reactive approach to flexible working requests might be negatively affected by the changes to the laws. Schools that continue to react to individual requests from a starting point of rejecting flexible working may find themselves firefighting an increasing number of requests and many hours of management time in dealing with them.

On the other hand, school leaders who take a proactive approach to flexible working are unlikely to notice much of an impact from the changes in the law. This might be because they already offer much of what the new legislation requires or because they use these changes as an opportunity to embrace flexible working and develop a more proactive approach to it. For example, a simple disruption to the status quo would be for a school to proactively ask all staff what they ideally want in terms of flexibility, at a set point in the academic year. This enables leaders to do most of the administration required to deal with requests in one go. Schools that do this are often surprised by how little people want. It might just be one late start a week to drop their own children off at school or the opportunity to join a staff meeting remotely rather than in person so they can be home to do a handover with a family member's carer. Some staff may want to reduce their hours; others already working part-time might want to increase their hours. Other staff may wish to stagger their retirement rather than leave altogether or work their management/Planning, Preparation and Assessment (PPA) time off site. Of course, there will be times when people don't know that they want/need flexibility at the point in time that leaders ask, but those individual requests can be dealt with as they come in. Asking everyone at once means that school leaders see the whole picture and puzzle together people's flexible working requests in a holistic way. This allows them to maximise staff wellbeing and their chances of retaining happy and effective staff, and highlights where there are gaps in skills or roles that need recruitment. The administrative burden of looking at whether flex can work is done all at once rather than every time a formal request comes in, so time is more efficiently and strategically spent working out how it might work in practice. This also increases the chances of leaders being able to say yes to support staff, teachers and leaders, thereby keeping them happy, productive and, importantly, in post. There is still no requirement to give everyone exactly what they want and it still must work for the school, and in cases where it doesn't, the answer can be no. This proactive approach which starts with wanting to make flexibility work, rather than a blank rejection, is not the traditional way of working in most schools but it should be the future. In the global recruitment crisis with 'Worldwide, 69 million teachers … needed to reach universal basic education by 2030' (Unesco, 2023: 1), all schools need to be more intentional about retaining staff:

> One simple and effective way is to ensure that the talented team you've already
> built stay with you by enabling them to develop their career within your
> school. This means providing a nurturing and supportive environment [which]
> they need to take the next step in their career while they remain in your
> school. (Tes Institute, 2023: 8)

Conclusion

I choose to be hopeful about the future of flexible working in the education sector, not least because moving forwards flexible working must be a priority. Schools need to retain and recruit the best staff, promote staff wellbeing and diversity, and may potentially need to streamline costs and maximise productive efficiency to cope with financial pressures. Flexible working can make a positive contribution to all these areas (Capita, n.d.).

Schools need to change how they view flexible working, not just because the law is changing, but also because they cannot afford not to capitalise on the benefits it brings.

Disruptions

- School leaders need to review how changes in the flexible working legislation will impact the policies and practices in their schools with regard to flexible working.
- Schools where the benefits of flexible working are not embraced should use this as an opportunity to explore how they can use flexible working for improved retention, recruitment, staff wellbeing, diversity and inclusion.
- Individual teachers and leaders who want to work more flexibly can use the opportunity of this legislative change to make requests for flexible working arrangements and open up a dialogue with their Headteachers.

- If you are a school leader, be brave about approaching flexible working positively. If you are hoping to work flexibly, be 10% Braver about requesting it, and if you are already working flexibly, be brave about setting boundaries and trailblazing in your school and share your progress with WomenEd and other schools.

References

Capita (n.d.) *Flexible working support in multi-academy trusts and schools* [Online]. Available at: www.flexibleworkingineducation.co.uk/ (accessed 18 October 2023].

Department for Business, Energy & Industrial Strategy (2021) *Making flexible working the default* [Online]. Available at: www.gov.uk/government/consultations/making-flexible-working-the-default (accessed 18 October 2023).

Department for Education (2023) *Get help with flexible working in schools* [Online]. Available at: www.gov.uk/guidance/get-help-with-flexible-working-in-schools (accessed 18 October 2023).

legislation.gov.uk (2023) *Employment Relations (Flexible Working) Act 2023* [Online]. Available at: www.legislation.gov.uk/ukpga/2023/33/contents/enacted (accessed 15 January 2024).

Pioneer Educational Trust (n.d.) *WorkWell & benefits package* [Online]. Available at: https://www.pioneereducationaltrust.org.uk/workwell/ (accessed 18 October 2023).

Tes Institute (2023) *Global teacher shortage: The rise in job vacancies* [Online]. Available at: www.tes.com/institute/blog/article/global-teacher-shortage-rise-job-vacancies (accessed 15 January 2024).

Unesco (2022) *World Teachers' Day: UNESCO sounds the alarm on the global teacher shortage crisis* [Online]. Available at: www.unesco.org/en/articles/world-teachers-day-unesco-sounds-alarm-global-teacher-shortage-crisis (accessed 15 January 2024).

21

MISCARRIAGE IS NOT A DIRTY WORD

WHY WE SHOULD NORMALISE TALKING ABOUT BABY LOSS

Esther Mustamu-Daniels

KEY POINTS

This chapter will:

- highlight that miscarriages are more common that many of us think
- ensure that personal experiences should be shared and not shied away from
- share how to support those experiencing loss
- be clear that policy and clarity make everyone's lives easier.

Introduction

Through this chapter, I share my personal journey with miscarriage and offer advice on how to help and support colleagues, employees or friends who may be going through the loss of a baby. I will ask you to query whether your organisation has a miscarriage policy and whether there are clear steps to support families experiencing or grieving such losses. I will also ask you to consider how you support someone who may have gone through or are going through any loss themselves.

Many factors can affect the impact of a loss and each situation is unique. When I began this chapter, I was extremely conflicted and conscious about writing about my own experiences. I didn't want to make assumptions about what others may have gone through or be going through or how people have coped, managed or processed their loss. However, the importance of awareness motivated me to be 10% braver. Despite how painful, raw and challenging the topic of miscarriage is to tackle, there is a need to understand, and dispel the silence and shame that often comes along with it. There is a need to ensure that, in the institutions where many of us spend so much of our time, a comprehensive and flexible framework of support is put in place in these situations, allowing anyone who may be going through the trauma of such a life-altering loss to get the comfort and support they require.

Miscarriage: What Does It Mean?

Miscarriage is the most common kind of pregnancy loss, affecting around one in four. There is mixed information around what exactly a miscarriage is and many people are unaware of just how prevalent miscarriages are. According to the NHS (NHS, n.d.) in the United Kingdom, one in eight pregnancies end in a miscarriage, while Tommy's, a UK-based, midwife-led website that provides advice for parents during and after pregnancy, suggests the numbers are more like one in five (Tommy's, 2023). March of Dimes, a US-based non-profit that works to improve the health of mothers and babies, states that one in four women in America experience a miscarriage in their lives (March of Dimes, 2023). The definition of what a miscarriage itself is differs from country to country. In some countries miscarriage is considered the loss of a foetus before 20 weeks, with any loss after this period labelled as a stillbirth. In other countries miscarriages are considered losses that occur up to 28 weeks and the term stillbirth is applied to any losses after this timeframe. This chapter is relevant to miscarriages in all its forms as well as molar and ectopic pregnancies and losses that occur after birth.

Personal Experiences

The dreams you had of holding your baby and watching them grow are gone. So much of what you wanted and planned for is lost. This can leave a large, empty space inside you. It may take a long time to heal this space.

As mentioned, miscarriages are so much more common than many people think. I had my first loss eight years ago and as I began to talk to others, I realised that many women around me had experienced the same thing, and that the shame, embarrassment and inadequacy I felt was also felt by them.

I started my family at a time that some would consider late. It took me some time to become pregnant, but joyously, at 30, I discovered I was pregnant and went on to have a relatively straightforward pregnancy experience. My daughter appeared to be making no effort to enter the world after the usual gestation period, so after 42 weeks, my labour was induced and she was born, a healthy, strong and absolutely beautiful baby. After a few years, my husband and I decided to try again and eventually I became pregnant. Excitedly, in expectation I began to ask myself the questions and make the plans that many families do at this time: Was I having a boy or a girl? When would I be due? When would I need to tell my employer? Where would the baby's room be? In the midst of all this, I went to hospital for a routine scan, still excited and believing everything was progressing as it should. The last thing that I expected was to hear the words which, at first, seemed to come from the doctor's mouth in a foreign language. I eventually realised I was being told that no heartbeat was being detected. The words hit me like a blow to my chest, a blow I don't think I have recovered from still. Unfortunately, I have had to hear those words four more times since then and the devastation is always immense. I had moved abroad since having my daughter, and so in all these instances, I didn't have the support of my extended family or close friends to help get me through. I was at a loss. My husband and I were forced to sit with the pain and grief, grief for not only the loss, but for everything that could have been.

Over the years I have had six pregnancies: one reached full term, four were missed miscarriages (before 12 weeks) and one miscarriage occurred in the second trimester. Each loss had its own emotions and challenges, and the anxiety before each scan and doctor's appointment increased dramatically in each instance. Rather than being able to rejoice and celebrate the discovery of each new pregnancy, each positive symbol on another pregnancy test led to massive amounts of fear and trepidation.

Through each miscarriage, each journey and each experience varied greatly, both in terms of how I felt personally and in terms of how I was supported by my colleagues and leaders in my place of employment. As leaders in a workplace, our actions, our knowledge and our empathy can have a profound impact on individuals and families who are going through any sort of loss. Miscarriage or pregnancy loss should not be taboo subjects. They are not subjects to shy away from or to be embarrassed about. Losses of this type can impact people very differently and each person's experience can vary. Based on the people I have spoken to, the multitude of stories available on sites such as The Miscarriage Association and the numerous groups I have been in contact with, support is crucial to processing, coping and healing in these situations.

There are many stories and shared experiences I read online in which I found great comfort. It was good to know that I was not alone and my feelings of anger, sometimes of inadequacy and sometimes of relief were not wrong; they did not make me a bad person and they were not something for which I should feel ashamed.

Women still face enormous stigma and shame when they lose a baby and they are often not encouraged to talk about their experience and loss. This can lead to isolation and disconnection, even from their partners and close family, and can lead to many women feeling trapped in their own personal grief. The stigma may be one that is felt internally and is often fuelled by cultural expectations; the expectation to be fertile and childbearing links to many women's sense of self-worth and self-esteem. Many of us feel the weight of the expectation for us, as women, to produce offspring for our families and be loving, nurturing mothers and if we are unable to do this, many of us feel incomplete. There can be, at times, shame and anger attached to this. Why did my body fail me?

Is there something wrong with me? Unwanted questions such as these can be hurtful, and when women going through such difficulties are asked questions by family or strangers such as why they don't have children or why they only have one, the pain felt is immense. Although unintentional, the sting of these words is felt in ways that the questioners will never understand.

Supporting Those Experiencing Loss

When someone you care about goes through a miscarriage, ectopic or molar pregnancy, it can be difficult to know how to support them, especially if you haven't been through it yourself. You may feel worried about saying or doing the wrong thing or be hesitant to bring it up in case it upsets them.

It is important to reiterate the fact that, like every pregnancy, every loss is different and each person experiencing loss will have different needs and different perspectives on their situation. As a supportive friend, colleague or leader, it is important to allow individuals to process their situation in the way of their choosing, but there are things that you can do to support and make things easier to work through.

Personally, regular check-ins helped me the most and validated my experience; knowing that someone cared made me feel like I wasn't going through it alone. They were the simplest and most caring method of showing support. Giving people time and space to process what they are going through can also be extremely important, as well as providing time for them to repair and heal physically and emotionally. While not wanting to talk about the topic may seem like the best and easiest approach, simply asking what people want is a good way to establish their needs and find out what you can do to help. This is where Human Resources (HR) or a school nurse can support greatly and operate as a point of contact for grieving individuals. Flexible working conditions, or a flexible approach to when and how you return to work and how you want colleagues to respond, help immensely.

If you are fortunate enough to have access to a counsellor, this could also be a very helpful option. The whole family may need support and if a family decides that this is something they'd like, counsellors, with their skills and knowledge, can prove invaluable. For me personally, I didn't realise there would be so many trigger points in my day-to-day experiences, such as receiving news about other pregnancies or seeing other pregnant women, seeing newborn babies, or seeing the date and realising it was a day I should have been having a routine check-up. Arriving at what would have been my expected due date for my second trimester miscarriage brought about a whole other form of trauma that I still struggle with. I had, and sometimes still have, emotional responses that are unexpected.

> My line manager has been amazing. I am so fortunate to have had her support and probably would not be in work now if it wasn't for her. (The Miscarriage Association, 2020)

In international education, many schools end up with employees whose spouses work in the same location and may even have children attending the institution too. In these instances, considering the whole family is crucial and each family member should be treated with care and sensitivity. My daughter has had to deal with losses at different stages of her development; with some she was unable to process the situation in its entirety. In our most challenging loss, she attended the funeral and held her baby brother before he was buried. It was not a situation that I wanted to put her through and I know that it impacted her greatly. Alongside obviously being able to talk to her father and I, she was offered the option of speaking to the school therapist and was also encouraged to speak to trusted teachers when she needed to.

My husband has also found our situation very challenging. While it is important that awareness be raised and support be given to women during miscarriages, mainly because of the huge physical and emotional trauma they must go through when a loss occurs, men in the family must also be recognised and supported. It can be very difficult for them to live up to cultural norms of being emotionally strong and providing support while having to process their loss and heartache themselves. Having a considerate work policy that allows men and/or women time to heal and time to support their partner's medical needs and doctors' appointments will help support and strengthen families as well as the institutions they work for.

The emotional toll and impact that this can have, as I keep mentioning, varies greatly depending on families and culture, and being aware of this and keeping an open and understanding dialogue with individuals going through this will always be greatly appreciated. It may be that a family wants complete privacy and does not want anyone to know what they have gone through, which of course should be respected and accommodated as much as possible. There are many places that offer advice and support with what to say and what not to say as sometimes, things and words we may think are helpful may not be received that way. Asking individuals what they need, educating oneself and leaning in with empathy and compassion will always yield the greatest results – even if this is done a little clumsily! Such displays of compassion are better than nothing at all. There are a multitude of excellent websites online that offer support, advice and leaflets.

Support and Policy in the Workspace

My managers knew how to help and it really did make going back to work so much easier. (The Miscarriage Association, n.d.a)

Having clarity and information around the process of loss is helpful for all. As a leader or someone supporting people experiencing loss, having a policy is extremely helpful to refer to and offer guidance.

The discrepancy linked to the definitions of what a miscarriage is can add to the confusion, so outlining what the definition is in your context is paramount, as the terminology impacts the process of aftercare and even the amount of maternity leave and time off one is entitled to. Knowing this provides a huge step forward for all parties involved in the process. Do consider how the country you reside in approaches the legalities linked to miscarriage and baby loss, but equally, also consider the mental wellbeing and care that you as an employer have the capacity to provide. The Miscarriage Association (n.d.b) offers a template policy and is encouraging organisations to pledge their support. Although it is based in the UK (where miscarriage is a protected characteristic as part of the 2010 Equality Act), parts of the policy can be adapted and used in any setting. Not only will it support those experiencing loss, it will also support managers and leaders to do their job with greater clarity. Some of the key aspects of the policy include:

- how to help
- communicating
- recording absence
- how to talk about it
- returning to work
- future leave.

The loss that any family experiences at any stage of a pregnancy is challenging and traumatic and there are numerous physical and mental strains placed on individuals. Often the pain and heartache can be long lasting and have an impact on wellbeing. With miscarriage and baby loss happening to so many, miscarriage must stop being treated as if it is a dirty word. We need to be brave and disrupt this narrative so we can support each other practically and emotionally.

> A vast range of responses – from intense grief to a practical shrug, from silence to openness, from sadness to acceptance – are all normal reactions, depending on personal experiences and cultural contexts. But while there are a variety of ways to respond to and process miscarriage, one thing is certain: Women everywhere can benefit from hearing one another's stories. (Kilshaw, 2017)

Disruptions

- Check that your organisation has a miscarriage policy in place and consider pledging your support linked to baby loss.
- Train wellbeing teams and leadership so that they are aware of how they can support a family experiencing any type of loss.
- Know how flexible working conditions can support your staff, both male and female, who are experiencing or have experienced loss.

References

Kilshaw, S. (2017) 'How culture shapes perceptions of miscarriage', *Sapiens*, 27 July [Online]. Available at: www.sapiens.org/biology/miscarriage-united-kingdom-qatar/ (accessed 22 March 2024).

March of Dimes (2023) *Miscarriage* [Online]. Available at: www.marchofdimes.org/find-support/topics/miscarriage-loss-grief/miscarriage (accessed 22 March 2024).

NHS (n.d.) *How common are miscarriages?* [Online]. Available at: www.nhs.uk/conditions/miscarriage/ (accessed October 2023).

The Miscarriage Association (2020) *Pregnancy loss and the workplace – a new resource.* Available at: www.miscarriageassociation.org.uk/blog/pregnancy-loss-and-the-workplace-a-new-resource/ (accessed 22 March 2024).

The Miscarriage Association (n.d.a) *Employees: information and support* [Online]. Available at www.miscarriageassociation.org.uk/miscarriage-and-the-workplace/employees-information-and-support/ (accessed 20 October 2023).

The Miscarriage Association (n.d.b) *A miscarriage policy*. Available at: www.miscarriageassociation.org.uk/miscarriage-and-the-workplace/human-resources-hr-information-and-support/a-miscarriage-policy/ (accessed 20 October 2023).

Tommy's (2023) *The baby loss series* [Online]. Available at: www.tommys.org/baby-loss-support/baby-loss-series (accessed 22 March 2024).

22

FINDING OPPORTUNITIES AND FREEDOM THROUGH FLEXIBLE WORKING

Helen Young

KEY POINTS

This chapter will:

- consider why part-time staff in schools are frequently seen as problematic and difficult
- argue that schools must be open to exploring the value of part-time staff
- show that staff shortages in UK schools could be alleviated through a consideration of flexible working.

Introduction

There are significant barriers to flexible working within many school environments. Within schools, flexible working often means part-time working. A recent report found that enabling part-time work in UK secondary schools seems to be particularly challenging (Sharp et al., 2019). School timetables are planned many months in advance and are complex in nature. The school day is fixed and doesn't easily lend itself to ad hoc variations in work patterns. However, some schools do manage to work around these obstacles.

The United Nations say that women carry out more than two and a half times more unpaid care work than men (UN Women, 2019). This means that women are more likely to request part-time work. Caroline Criado-Perez suggests that 'a workplace predicated on the assumption that a worker can come into work every day, at times and locations that are wholly unrelated to the location or opening hours of schools, child-care centres, doctors and grocery stores, simply doesn't work for women. It hasn't been designed to' (2019).

Schools are also increasingly facing staff shortages. Studies in the UK show that teacher recruitment is failing to keep up with increasing pupil numbers and that retention of existing teachers is getting worse over time (Belger, 2023). Chapter 14 highlights these shortages are global. Secondary schools require set numbers of staff with subject expertise, which is determined by the demand for courses. This puts pressure on so-called shortage subjects, which means that Headteachers do not always consider staff requests for reduced hours from teachers of such subjects.

Many schools have outdated views, seeing part-time staff as a problem rather than an opportunity. In my experience, having worked in schools for 25 years, women with childcare needs, and therefore specific requirements, are more likely to have requests for part-time work turned down.

Yes, But There's No Demand …

NFER data shows women make up 63% of all workers within secondary schools in the UK (Sharp et al., 2019). The same report found that only 19% of all teachers work part-time, which is much lower than the average of 36% of women in other sectors. This data suggests that demand for part-time work is being unmet.

Recent research in the UK found that many teachers leave the profession due to a lack of flexibility in working hours (Worth et al., 2018). Furthermore, the Department for Education (2019) in England suggest that teachers taking a career break are far less likely to return to the profession due to the lack of flexible working (Department for Education, 2019).

In many other sectors of industry, part-time and flexible working is considered more acceptable and even valuable in terms of recruitment, retention and wellbeing. By contrast, schools, which have a largely female-dominated workforce, still have a relatively low proportion of part-time workers (Timewise, 2022). The success of the four-day week trial in the UK has set a precedent for moves towards a better work and life balance (Stewart, 2023). Following the trial, over 90% of businesses said they intended to continue with the four-day week. Two schools in the UK are trialling a version of a four-day week to boost recruitment and retention and we look forward to what they learn.

The Benefits of Part-Time Teachers

There are around 1.5 million people working in UK schools and over 9 million students. The benefits of staff working part-time or accessing flexible practices are therefore huge, potentially affecting just over 15% of the country's population:

- Flexible working is intended to promote a happier, loyal, and more productive workforce, and therefore benefit both employees and employers alike
- Flexible working … could encourage talented job-seekers to work for a particular company
- It can help enable employers to avoid redundancies
- It shows that a company is progressive and listening to the needs of its staff
- Employees can save on commuting time and costs
- A more diverse workforce is possible
- Modern technology means remote working is far more achievable now than ever before. (Morgan McKinley, 2019)

Why Is It Needed in Education?

Teaching is frequently acknowledged as one of the most stressful jobs. The anonymous app 'Teacher Tapp' analysed teacher burnout over time (Ford, 2022) and found a correlation between teacher sickness rates and contact hours with students. Those 'teaching 70 pupils or fewer were most likely to have zero burnout feelings', whereas one-third of people teaching more than 300 pupils each week had either 'persistent or complete burnout'. If fewer contact hours lead to lower levels of burnout and absence, we can assume that part-time staff are more likely to experience lower levels of stress and absence. This reduces staff costs and is beneficial to students, who are more likely to experience consistency.

Working part-time shouldn't just be about reducing the negatives. There are many positives to part-time work, such as greater communication and connection outside of the school environment. This could be from a personal perspective or could even benefit the school. In my experience, one advantage is the opportunity to network, read, plan, and strengthen the school's links with external organisations. I don't mean working when not being paid to work; it's more about the opportunities that come with the additional time away from work, and lower levels of stress and fatigue. I'll come back to this later in this chapter.

The Barriers to Part-Time Working

Working part-time isn't always easy. I've worked part-time for over 20 years and, in my experience, many of the issues highlighted above persist. School leaders often fail to appreciate that part-time staff are paid less and should carry out proportionally fewer tasks. Part-time staff often attend more meetings, duties and training than they are paid to do. They are often required to carry out the same leadership role, but in less time and with less money which WomenEd and Flex Teach Talent campaign to address. They may carry out fieldwork and additional duties during their time off, but don't feel that they can request payment for them. It takes a strong person to question the status quo, and as part-time staff are disproportionately female, resisting additional tasks can be seen as being difficult by leaders rather than being assertive. Smith et al. (2018) find that male leaders were described using only two negative terms, whilst their female counterparts were described using a wide range of negative words such as inept, frivolous, excitable, temperamental and panicky.

The penalties for part-time working are clear to see. Lower pay and pension are inevitable, but fewer opportunities and lower status can exacerbate the financial impact. Whilst this is an issue for both men and women, the Trades Union Congress (TUC, 2022) found that women are more likely than men to take part in flexible working arrangements that result in a loss of time and money.

Speaking to staff from different schools, there are common attitudes towards part-time staff. Talk of demotion in exchange for a part-time contract is common. Nat Wilcox and Lucy Hemsley discussed this in their 'Leadership Journey' presentation for WomenEd South West, England in 2021. They shared things that they'd been told, such as 'you can't be a senior leader at a secondary school and work part-time' and 'if you want to progress with your career, you will need to return to work full time after maternity leave'.

My Liberation from Full-Time Work

Early in my career, I recognised that teaching was detrimental to my work–life balance. I went to work at the head offices of a UK bank. Whilst away from the classroom, I had the idea of teaching part-time. At the time, my reduction in salary was negligible and felt like a compromise I was happy to make. I returned to the profession, applying and gaining an interview for a role that was full-time with responsibility, but I stated that I wanted to work part-time. At the time, I was in a stable job and I felt that I had nothing to lose from my request. Upon arrival, I was met with conflicting views about my part-time request. The Headteacher wanted to fill the role regardless, but my line manager didn't believe that the job could be done by a part-time member of staff. It was evident that the only other applicant was unsuitable for the role, but that my request was causing problems. I was asked about my reason for requesting part-time and my answers were met with a degree of shock and distrust; as a female with no children or other responsibilities, it was incomprehensible that I would work part-time. Despite this, I was offered the job.

Working part-time has given me an asset that has been invaluable to my career progression and personal wellbeing. This asset is time. I have been successful in many roles that sound impressive and attractive to prospective employers. This is because I have time, and with time comes opportunities and freedom. I have had time to find out about new opportunities and to think, and the importance of this should not be underestimated.

One example of this was just over 20 years ago, when a large media company visited my school, looking for volunteers to take part in a project. It sounded interesting and I immediately said yes. I was the only person who took up this opportunity; nobody else had the time. I carried out the work in my own time and enjoyed it. Within a month,

I was on the media company's payroll. This was a defining moment in my career, and arguably my life in general.

Later in my career, I was relocating and looking to move schools again. There were no part-time roles available, but by this point I was carrying out a range of consultancy roles alongside teaching, which meant that I had a network of contacts and a degree of credibility that couldn't have been acquired from the classroom alone. A local school readily offered me a part-time role. Upon arrival at the school, it became clear that part-time staff were not usually employed. The irony of a school that didn't appear to 'like' part-time workers, employing a part-time worker for the skills and experience she'd gained through working part-time, was not lost on me.

Conclusion

At a national level, the government provides guidance to encourage schools and multi-academy trusts to adopt flexible working (GOV.UK, 2022). Despite this, Lough (2019) shows that over one quarter of teacher requests for part-time work are being turned down. The correlation between contact hours and burnout is clear and, regardless of the human impact, a matter of basic economics. Nationally, vast sums of money are spent advertising teaching to young trainees, when many established members of staff may remain in post if their requests to work flexibly are considered. This is unsustainable and uneconomical.

Progress is being made. WomenEd have worked hard to raise awareness of flexible working in schools, through presentations, blogs, conferences, podcasts and books (*10% Braver: Inspiring Women to Lead Education* [2019]), and contributes to the Department for Education (England) Working Party on Flexible Working. Members of the WomenEd community have written specific books on flexible working and highlight the need for part-time teachers with responsibility to receive full salary for the responsibility, which needs to happen. Inequity of pay, respect and career development must have no place in our schools for those working flexibly and schools should embrace a diverse workforce in all its glory.

Disruptions

School leaders must:

- Recognise the benefits of part-time staff. Activities taking place outside of school, both socially and professionally, can add value within school.
- Value existing part-time staff by ensuring that they carry out duties and attend meetings proportionate to their contracted hours.
- Facilitate remote training, allowing full- and part-time staff to work more flexibly.
- Accommodate flexible working by considering requests for part-time work, or trusting staff to work at home during protected non-contact time.

References

Belger, T. (2023) 'In short supply: Cover costs soar as teacher shortages and illness bite', *schoolsweek*, 10 January [Online]. Available at: https://schoolsweek.co.uk/school-supply-teachers-illness-cover-recruitment (accessed 10 June 2023).

Criado-Perez, C. (2019) *Invisible Women: Exposing Data Bias in a World Designed for Men.* London: Vintage Digital.

Department for Education (2019) *Exploring flexible working practice in schools* [Online]. Available at: https://assets.publishing.service.gov.uk/government/uploads/system/uploads/attachment_data/file/938786/Exploring_flexible_working_practice_in_schools_-_lit_review.pdf (accessed 8 June 2023).

Ford, I. (2022) *Are things getting better or worse? Crying, burnout, behaviour and the menopause!* [Online]. Available at: https://teachertapp.co.uk/articles/are-things-getting-better-or-worse-crying-burnout-behaviour-and-the-menopause/ (accessed 1 June 2023).

GOV.UK (2022) *Flexible working in schools* [Online]. Available at: www.gov.uk/government/publications/flexible-working-in-schools/flexible-working-in-schools--2 (accessed 10 June 2023).

Lough, C. (2019) 'Over quarter of headteachers refuse part-time requests', *Tes Magazine*, 21 June [Online]. Available at: www.tes.com/magazine/archive/over-quarter-headteachers-refuse-part-time-requests (accessed 10 June 2023).

Morgan Mckinley (2019) 'Flexible Working: The Real Pros and Cons', 6 January [Online]. Available at: https://www.morganmckinley.com/uk/article/flexible-working-real-pros-and-cons (accessed 10 May 2024).

Sharp, C., Smith, R., Worth, J. and Van den Brande, J. (2019) *Part-Time Teaching and Flexible Working in Secondary Schools.* Slough: NFER.

Smith, D. G., Rosenstein, J. E. and Nikolov, M. C. (2018) 'The different words we use to describe male and female leaders', *Harvard Business Review*, 25 May [Online]. Available at: https://hbr.org/2018/05/the-different-words-we-use-to-describe-male-and-female-leaders (accessed 21 August 2023).

Stewart, H. (2023) 'Four-day week: "Major breakthrough" as most UK firms in trial extend changes', *The Guardian*, 21 February [Online]. Available at: www.theguardian.com/money/2023/feb/21/four-day-week-uk-trial-success-pattern. (accessed 10 June 2023).

Timewise (2022) *Developing a whole-school approach to flexible working* [Online]. Available at: https://timewise.co.uk/wp-content/uploads/2022/03/Developing-a-whole-school-approach-to-flexible-working.pdf (accessed 10 June 2023).

TUC (2022) *Women much more likely than men to have flexible work arrangements that lead to loss of hours and pay* [Online]. Available at: www.tuc.org.uk/news/tuc-women-much-more-likely-men-have-flexible-work-arrangements-lead-loss-hours-and-pay (accessed 8 June 2023).

UN Women (2019) *Redistribute unpaid work* [Online]. Available at: www.unwomen.org/en/news/in-focus/csw61/redistribute-unpaid-work (accessed 1 June 2023).

Wilcox, N. [@redhappyshoes] (2021) 27 November [Twitter]. Available at: https://twitter.com/redhappyshoes/status/1464543655549673481 (accessed 10 June 2023).

Worth, J., Lynch, S., Hillary, J., Rennie, C. and Andrade, J. (2018) *Teacher workforce dynamics in England: Nurturing, supporting and valuing teachers* [Online]. Available at: www.nfer.ac.uk/media/3111/teacher_workforce_dynamics_in_england_final_report.pdf (accessed 10 June 2023).

23

IS THERE A PARENTAL PENALTY IN EDUCATION?

Hannah Duncan

KEY POINTS

This chapter will:

- discuss a well-documented motherhood penalty in education in England
- argue that male parent–teachers are penalised due to losing out on time with their young children
- disrupt the status quo to normalise flexible working patterns and caring responsibilities for *all* teachers and leaders which will support equality in education.

Introduction

Personal experience leads me to answer the question 'Is there a parental penalty in education?' with an emphatic 'Yes!'. Unsurprisingly, as a young mother and teacher in England I have been affected by the motherhood penalty. Early in my career I took up a music development opportunity. When the school became aware of my first pregnancy, I was contacted by course leaders to say they were sorry I was unable to continue due to personal issues, but they would send me resources from the remaining sessions if I was interested. I was shocked. Who had said this on my behalf and without even consulting me? I was also outraged, though it didn't occur to me that this was potentially unlawful, amounting to unfavourable treatment and discrimination due to my pregnancy. I had to be 10% braver and advocate for myself and the school did allow me to complete the course, which is one of the most impactful development opportunities I have undertaken. This was the first of several instances where my career in education was negatively affected because I was a mother. This is my experience in England, and WomenEd also explores this as a global issue.

Not Just a Motherhood Penalty

My experience is not unusual, the motherhood penalty in education is well documented (Sheppard, 2022). In a profession where 76% of teachers are women (UK Government, 2023), this focus on the motherhood penalty is a fundamental part of the equation when looking at the wellbeing and sustainability of the teaching profession. Furthermore, developing an understanding of the experiences of being a mother–teacher is justifiable when female teachers aged 30–39 are the biggest demographic to leave teaching each year (ibid.). But if we are to change things for mother–teachers we need to see our teaching profession as a united community of practitioners. I don't mean to diminish the impact of the motherhood penalty on women in education, but without male allies and everyone working together to challenge the dominant narratives around motherhood (e.g. it is the mother's responsibility to put caring first and work second, to deal with birthday parties, play dates and the washing …), we will struggle to disrupt anything further than we have achieved already. We should perhaps be using the term 'parental penalty' instead as it is more equal and inclusive. It acknowledges different family configurations, such as same-sex couples. The term 'parental penalty' also acknowledges that male teachers who are fathers are affected. Women and men are affected differently by this parental penalty: women in terms of achieving career progression and equitable pay, men through lack of opportunities for engaging in caring roles and working flexibly. So both genders should be considered in this campaign for gender equality in education. Both genders need to work collaboratively to achieve this aim for successful, lasting change to occur.

There are some male teachers who work flexibly or take more than their statutory two weeks of paternity leave in England. However, we know very little about their experiences and how this may, or may not, affect their pay and career progression. This is the topic of my PhD research and I hope to find out how father–teachers are affected by their active challenge to 'normal' and 'expected' gender divisions of labour and caring roles.

Additionally, there is an aspect of the motherhood penalty that is often overlooked: we know that a gender wage gap exists (WomenEd, 2023) but we usually discuss it from the perspective of women being held back. However, we must not forget to challenge the fatherhood bonus (Cory and Stirling, 2016). It is a double injustice that men who become fathers and maintain a full-time traditional working pattern not only seem to avoid a parental penalty in terms of pay but are rewarded for becoming a parent. In fact, in some professions, fatherhood is seen as a valued characteristic of employees as it is thought to demonstrate greater work commitment, stability and deservingness. For most men the fact of fatherhood results in a wage bonus; for most women motherhood results in a wage penalty (Budig, 2014). While the gender pay gap has been decreasing, the pay gap related to parenthood is increasing. Are we mothers not deserving of our professional roles and wages too?

Make Your Partner a Real Partner: Getting to 50/50

With everything seemingly stacked against mother–teachers, it can seem impossible to challenge and disrupt the status quo. But Sandberg as well as Meers and Strober provide some solutions that apply to education as much as any other sector. In 2010 Sheryl Sandberg (then COO of Facebook) gave a TED Talk looking at why there are too few women leaders. One of her key solutions for women was that they needed to 'make their partner a real partner' (Sandberg, 2010). However, it is not as simple as it sounds. This is because it involves both women and men being 10% braver and having the confidence to disrupt the embedded gender practices, behaviours and beliefs that are entrenched in many societies and educational institutions. In the workplace this means father–teachers need to be clear that they too have caring responsibilities and might need to stay home when a child is sick or be the one who leaves 'on time' at the end of the school day to do a nursery or school pick-up. In the home the challenge is two-fold. Mothers need to let go and accept that things might be done differently. And fathers need to share the load mentally as well as physically, supporting their partners with organising childcare or packing the bags the night before so that both partners have the capacity to fulfil their professional and caring roles.

Meers and Strober (2013) present the same idea in a different way. They suggest that there is a constantly shifting balance between caring and professional roles for each partner in a two-person household. A new mother on maternity leave might take on 90% of the caring responsibilities. Assuming she returns to work, this balance might shift to a more equal 60/40 divide of the caring role and work towards an equal 50/50 split of household, caring role and professional, wage-earning role. The key point here is that both partners see themselves as a team. This requires us all to challenge our own beliefs and identities. Regardless of gender or working patterns, both partners should try to consider themselves as carers *and* professionals with neither role being more important than the other because a person is a particular gender.

Levelling the Hierarchies

Meers and Strober (2013) offer another concept which is very useful in helping us to visualise the challenges we face. Traditional gender practices and institutional arrangements often mean that men are viewed as first-class citizens in the workplace, with women, in particular mothers, being seen as second-class citizens. This is especially true of mothers – who often work part-time or flexibly – due to the pervasive narrative that part-time work is inferior, and mothers are therefore considered to be less committed to their professional roles (Meers and Strober, 2013). In the home these statuses are often reversed. We need to disrupt these gender hierarchies in both the workplace and our homes if we are going to support equality in the education sector and support all our parent–teachers.

My husband now jokes that his status as a first-class citizen in the home is evidenced when he returns from the weekly shop having picked up something that was not on the shopping list but which he noticed was running low in the house. He also picks up the children from school and nursery one day a week for which he had to put in a flexible working request. It might seem a small step, but with the larger effect of showing his school that he has a family and caring responsibilities which he values and wants to prioritise. It also allows me to work a full day and not have to leave at 14:30 to do the school run, then make up the hours in the evening when the children are in bed.

Conclusion

Fathers in England are increasingly spending more hours with their children than in any previous generation (Bataille and Hyland, 2022; Burgess et al., 2022). This shows they want to take a more active role in the upbringing of their own children and are currently being penalised in the education sector by not having the same access to Shared Parental Leave or extended, paid Paternity Leave that many other sectors now offer. In supporting our father–teachers to have the confidence to put in those flexible working requests, to take the time off to care for unwell children and to fight their own battles to overcome the male parental penalty, the conditions for mother–teachers will also improve. By levelling the hierarchies in both the home and our educational institutions we change the narrative around commitment, part-time working and a gendered divide of working/caring roles. When we stop viewing part-time workers as second-class citizens, we may find that the gender pay gap for parents starts to reduce, women teachers can progress more easily into senior and executive leadership roles and fathers start to proudly talk about their caring responsibilities and the support they offer their partners.

Disruptions

- Be 10% braver and ask for the Shared Parental Leave policy or push for one to be written.
- Negotiate enhanced pay for Paternity Leave and look to extend it beyond the statutory two weeks given in England; pave the way for others to make use of different parental leave models.
- Challenge others in school who speak negatively about parent–teachers taking time off or leaving 'on time'. Don't allow them to perpetuate gender biases.
- Speak positively about flexible and part-time colleagues and working patterns. Help to usualise it for *all*, which will in turn help reduce the parental penalty in education.

References

Bataille, C. D. and Hyland, E. (2022) 'Involved fathering: How new dads are redefining fatherhood', *Personnel Review*, *52*(4), 1010–1032.

Budig, M. J. (2014) *The Fatherhood Bonus and the Motherhood Penalty: Parenthood and the gender gap in pay* [Online]. Available at: www.thirdway.org/report/the-fatherhood-bonus-and-the-motherhood-penalty-parenthood-and-the-gender-gap-in-pay (accessed 27 October 2023).

Burgess, A., Goldman, R. and Davies, J. (2022) *Closing the gap: UK working fathers' and mothers' use of time 2014–22* [Online]. Available at: www.fatherhoodinstitute.org/wp-content/uploads/2022/12/Closing-the-Gap-Report.pdf. (accessed 27 October 2023).

Cory, G. and Stirling, A. (2016) *Pay and Parenthood: An Analysis of Wage Inequality Between Mums and Dads*. London: Trades Union Congress [Online]. Available at: www.tuc.org.uk/sites/default/files/Pay_and_Parenthood_Touchstone_Extra_2016_LR.pdf (accessed 25 March 2024).

Meers, S. and Strober, J. (2013) *Getting to 50/50: How Working Couples Can Have It All by Sharing It All*. London: Piatkus.

Sandberg, S. (2010) 'Why we have too few women leaders', *YouTube*, December [Online]. Available at: https://www.ted.com/talks/sheryl_sandberg_why_we_have_too_few_women_leaders (accessed 30 April, 2024).

Sheppard, E. (ed.) (2022) *A Guide to Teaching, Parenting and Creating Family Friendly Schools: The Maternityteacher Paternityteacher Project Handbook*. London: Routledge.

UK Government (2023) *School workforce in England* [Online]. Available at: https://explore-education-statistics.service.gov.uk/find-statistics/school-workforce-in-england (accessed 27 October 2023).

WomenEd (2023) *Gender pay gap campaign* [Online]. Available at: https://womened.com/gender-pay-gap-campaign (accessed 27 October 2023).

24

MAKING MORE OF MENOPAUSE

Derry Richardson

KEY POINTS

This chapter will:

- share how menopause gripped me at my time to shine and how being 10% braver helped me to survive and thrive
- offer useful tips on how to manage your own symptoms and let you know you are part of a community of change
- challenge you to take the lead in shaping a more flexible work environment where menopause and perimenopause are appreciated and understood by our peers and leaders, so enabling women to flourish.

Introduction

Hot flushes and lack of sleep had me questioning my performance, my ability to lead and my ambition. Beginning hormone replacement therapy (HRT) was a big step for me, although there is ongoing controversy against the various drugs and combinations available. Despite this, the relief to my suffering is thanks to brave women before me who disrupted the narrative and brought menopause and perimenopause to the forefront for all women.

However, this leap into the unknown pales into insignificance against some of the professional opportunities I have sought in my career through motherhood, family demands and health scares – from leaving the classroom to becoming an adviser, diving headfirst into the world of education publishing, setting up my own consultancy, authoring, and most recently taking on a senior role in local authority. Being a professional woman has demands which I did not realise would challenge and build my confidence.

At 37 I took on a new role in education publishing at five months pregnant, starting only a few weeks before the birth of my second son. Unfortunately, life has a way of testing you at the most critical moments, and this euphoric event was quickly consumed by a cancer scare which redressed the balance of my personal and professional life in ways I could not have imagined. The women leaders around me at this time put faith in me succeeding in a new and promoted role. They waited the expected three months for me to return from maternity, then for my health to improve. Crucially they provided a work environment to return to which enabled me to thrive. Despite the setbacks, balance of motherhood, and professional advancement, I knew I had more to say, more to give, more to learn. To shape my own leadership style, working with and for inspirational role models in education and educational publishing, was a driving force which propelled me on.

What I did not expect while juggling motherhood, being a wife, extensive travel and managing my own expectations, was being struck down by hot flushes in my early forties. The creeping sensation began like ants scurrying across my skin, leading to the uncontrollable urge to whip off clothes and stand in the rain. Not ideal, of course, when leading a meeting, presenting online live, trying to persuade others that your direction is the right direction.

I struggled at first. I felt out of control and as though my personal appearance was being scrutinised. I found dressing for events difficult. My hair began to go limp and awkward to style for being 'on show'. My confidence dipped, and my usual eagerness to be involved, to have an opinion or take on a challenge deflated. If motherhood had not held back my career, then the decline of my body and changes in hormones was not going to. We must talk about what is happening. We must seek advice and support in the workplace. We must take back control. We must be 10% Braver.

Thanks to flexible working and a hybrid approach (before Covid), I was able to manage my time. I realised this change was not temporary, but a change I needed to embrace and learn more about. So I researched, questioned, considered, and decided that either I owned it, or it was going to own me. I used my perimenopause as a new superpower.

What Are Menopause and Perimenopause?

Menopause and perimenopause are better understood by society, but far from integrated and valued as a protected characteristic in policy. This means that managing and leading through menopause and perimenopause remains a struggle for women at key stages in their professional life. The 2021 study conducted by University of Central London and published in *Social Science & Medicine* (Bryson et al., 2022) explains the symptoms of menopause and perimenopause as:

> many and varied, and include sweats, joint aches and pains, hot flushes, night sweats, trouble sleeping, fatigue, palpitations, dizziness, severe headaches and

migraines, irritability and mood swings, anxiety and depression, tearfulness, panic, forgetfulness and poor concentration.

I can relate to these, with the most unbearable to me as a leader being forgetfulness and poor concentration. Much of my suffering happened behind closed doors, and I found ways to manage symptoms early on. I would enter meetings prepped and ready to drive change and lead my team through challenge; then the anxiety overwhelmed me, the sweat reared its head and began running uncontrollably down the spine, over the hairline, threatening to leave awkward sweat marks on my carefully chosen outfit, my hair screaming at me to pin it up and anxiety crippling the well-balanced words I had prepared. These are mental and physical symptoms which challenged my professionalism and manifested in self-doubt.

So, with my mind racing to grasp onto the thread, recognising the preoccupation with my symptoms about to take over, what did I do? I stopped.

How to Manage Menopause and Perimenopause

In education it is not always easy to stop. We are a complex profession, some governed by the school timetable, others through travel and exposure to wide audiences, many working with male colleagues in roles of seniority or perceived power. As women experiencing crippling effects of menopause and perimenopause, we can be better informed to take control and support our workplace to work with us, not against us.

Own your superpower:

- know that it is ok to stop, physically and mentally
- build an environment where you matter and explaining this to others can liberate you
- understand your rights
- own it – menopause and perimenopause are part of who you are, and you can do remarkable things
- preparation is the key to success – start your day assuming you will need to change direction or stop.

Lead organisational change:

- request reasonable adjustments to work schedules or timetables
- model effective flexible working options
- use your employee assistance scheme.

Take personal responsibility:

- talk about what is happening to you and how it affects your ability to perform at your absolute best all the time

- understand better how each symptom manifests itself through you and create a tool kit which helps you manage
- talk to your General Practitioner and use any relevant regional guidelines to support your conversations and to achieve the results you want – an example is guidelines produced by NICE (2019)
- identify who your trusted colleague or professional friend will be – their role will be to support you and ensure there are no risks to you leaving your post temporarily, to feature in reasonable working adjustments, and remind you that you do not need to suffer in silence
- breathe (properly).

Breathing techniques have proven a simple and quick way to calm and slow the onset of anxiety or sweats and gave me time to make my excuses, or find someone to step in, and save my dignity. Having spoken to my manager and been honest in that I may need to be away from my post/role with little or no warning reduced some of the stress. Working on a risk assessment to mitigate the impact my absence may cause was reflective and positive for my teams and management. I found that reducing the anxiety that I may not cope with or would be embarrassed by the symptoms helped control them. Do not be ashamed of being a woman. Be proud of what you have achieved, what you do and how you cope, sometimes in extraordinary circumstances.

What Can We Do to Change How Menopause and Perimenopause Are Managed in Our Workplace?

I was honest. I asked for time to address my personal needs (a toilet run, a change of top, to stand in the fresh air and simply breathe). I found humour a way to acknowledge what had been crippling effects of perimenopause. I carried a fan; I wore my hair up and had it cut. I planned my time so that I had breaks and opportunities to decompress to perform at my best when it mattered most. I found a trusted colleague with whom I could work to mitigate the risks associated with needing to step away from my position at times (leaving learners, a meeting, or critical conversation).

Research from University College London, conducted in 2021, illustrates not only the immediate impact on women suffering with symptoms of menopause and peri-menopause but begins to tell the story of longer-term impacts (Sullivan, 2022). The study concludes that the onset of menopause before age 45 reduces months spent in work by 9%, around 4 months' employment, for women during their early fifties. The implications may be women unable to progress, seek promotion, sustain long-term careers and a sense of self-worth and professional satisfaction.

In 2022, the Department of Work and Pensions published a new policy paper *Menopause and the Workplace: How to Enable Fulfilling Working Lives: Government Response.* This central change in emphasis for the United Kingdom suggests an irreversible advance, 'working with employer groups to understand how we can promote best practice for supporting people experiencing the menopause at work' … 'with the aim of improving the experience of employees experiencing difficult menopausal symptoms in the workplace' (2022: 17).

It goes on to suggest that 'menopause is not a protected characteristic in the Equality Act 2010 (the Act), but sex, age and disability are all characteristics which provide protection against unfair treatment of employees going through the menopause' (2022: 6). Menopause and perimenopause are no longer taboo, but far from understood by all. In a profession which consistently reports to be at around 70%+ female, do you work with a policy that appreciates your characteristics?

Deborah Garlick, Founder of Henpicked, explains that: 'There is no denying some menopausal symptoms can be tough. But by seeking help and support, there is no longer any reason for them to affect your career satisfaction and capability at work.' The UK Department of Health and Social Care Government's 2022–23 guidelines (2022) to NHS England suggest it is 'important to foster an open and inclusive culture where colleagues experiencing symptoms of the menopause feel they can talk openly about their experiences and receive or be signposted to the support they need' (2022: 9).

It can seem a daunting prospect asking for help, especially in leadership roles. But with WomenEd behind you, feel empowered to disrupt the norm.

Disruptions: Advocate for Flexible Working Practices

- Be part of a *change* we can evidence. Lead on the development of policy referring to research and evidence to inform change.
- *Challenge* your own role in advancing research into the effects of menopause and perimenopause in the workplace. Consider how your own experience can benefit future research and data leading to international change and recognition.
- Have the *confidence* to drive change, for you and our WomenEd *community* worldwide. Set up a menopause and perimenopause group which can collectively address the issue within your workplace.
- *Collaborate* with others to share learning, successful disruption, and positive outcomes for women seeking flexible working solutions to perimenopause and menopausal suffering.
- Make *connections* with those who can empower you, those who will understand you, and those who will champion you, personally and professionally.
- Use the research and knowledge on our WomenEd's health page on our website: https://womened.com/campaigns-resources/womens-health-in-education-work
- *Communicate* with *clarity* and conviction what you need in order to be successful:

  ○ ask to see your employer's policy on flexible working
  ○ ask to see your employer's policy for reasonable adjustments
  ○ ask if you have a policy on menopause (If they do not have one, write it!).

References

Bryson, A., Conti, G., Hardy, R., Peycheva, D. and Sullivan, A. (2022) 'The consequences of early menopause and menopause symptoms for labour market participation', *Social Science & Medicine*, 293(5): 114676 .

Department of Health and Social Care (2022) *The Government's 2022–23 mandate to NHS England* [Online]. Available at: https://assets.publishing.service.gov.uk/government/uploads/system/uploads/attachment_data/file/1065713/2022-to-2023-nhs-england-mandate.pdf (accessed 15 January 2024).

Department of Work and Pensions (DWP) (2022) *Menopause and the Workplace: How to Enable Fulfilling Working Lives: Government Response*. London: DWP.

Garlick, D. (2020) 'What to do when menopause is affecting your work', *Henpicked*, 2 June [Online]. Available at: www.henpicked.net/menopause-hub (accessed July 2023).

National Institute for Health and Care Excellence (NICE) (2019) *Menopause: Diagnosis and management guideline* [Online]. Available at: www.nice.org.uk/guidance/ng23 (accessed July 2023).

Sullivan, A. (2022) 'Women who experience early menopause spend 4 months fewer in work during their early 50s', *University College London*, 24 January [Online]. Available at: https://www.ucl.ac.uk/ioe/news/2022/jan/women-who-experience-early-menopause-spend-4-months-fewer-work-during-their-early-50s (accessed 20 April 2024).

25

MENOPAUSE AND FLEXIBLE WORKING

STARTING CONVERSATIONS

Suzanne Brown and Katy Marsh-Davies

KEY POINTS

This chapter will:

- explore the global teacher recruitment and retention crisis which includes losing experienced and talented women teachers in mid-life
- understand that menopause is a normal life stage usually impacting on women in mid-life. We acknowledge that trans and non-binary people may also undergo menopause. It can occur at any time following the start of periods, naturally or due to surgical/medical interventions
- discuss flexible working as a possible way to support women in managing their symptoms – but it doesn't come without costs
- advocate for policies and cultures which encourage conversations about menopause and promote genuinely flexible ways of working.

Introduction

Hot and sweaty, anxious, and muddled, words and names eluding you, exhausted from poor sleep, possibly bleeding heavily, but unable to able to check because you can't leave the children in your classroom unattended. All this on top of looking after your own children and worrying about your parents' health. It sounds like you might be a teacher experiencing the menopause transition!

For some women, flexible working – possibly part-time – might seem the only way of managing menopausal symptoms, despite the negative financial and career implications. But is it? In this chapter we consider the evidence for why this decision should not be taken lightly. We raise awareness of how more than a reduced salary may be at stake, for both individuals and for the profession more widely. In this chapter we advocate for conversations to take place as part of changing policies and cultures around menopause and flexible working in schools. We are grateful to our research assistant Sydney Baker for her support.

Teachers and Menopause

Whilst around 25% of women do not experience menopausal symptoms beyond the cessation of periods, the majority will, and for 25% of these, the symptoms are debilitating (British Menopause Society, 2021). Perimenopausal symptoms, which are wide-ranging, and can include anxiety, heavy bleeding, loss of confidence, and distracting hot flushes (Brewis et al., 2017; Steffan, 2021), can occur for up to ten years before menopause. This can be particularly problematic for teachers who are in front of the class and who cannot leave the room easily.

The story of Sarah, a Headteacher (cited in Education Support, 2023: paragraph 8), reveals how women in leadership can also be affected.

> At the beginning of 2020, I found that on top of forgetfulness, I started to have the dreaded hot flushes at night, which impacted on how much sleep I was getting. I was also suffering with chronic diarrhoea …
>
> … The real climax came with the crippling anxiety that I started to feel at all times of day and night. I spent hours questioning my ability to do my job, be a good mum, partner and friend – I felt like I couldn't do anything anymore and felt that I lost who I really was. After a particularly stressful day, I went home to bed and literally stayed there for days …

Replies to this post affirm and highlight such struggles, including feelings of being overwhelmed and thinking about leaving the profession on a daily basis due to the impacts of menopause on physical and mental health.

Across the wider UK workforce, ten percent of women who work during their menopause transition leave their jobs due to symptoms (Bazeley et al., 2022). This is particularly pertinent for the teaching profession where women make up the majority of the workforce (OECD, 2021). Sharon MacArthur's article (2021) makes the following important point: 'Women are suffering in silence, and considering leaving their jobs, which is bad news for a profession like teaching which struggles to recruit and retain talented staff.'

The perilous state of teacher recruitment and retention (Worth, 2023) means we cannot afford the loss of experienced and talented teachers due to a perfectly normal stage of a woman's life being inadequately supported. Changing this situation not only would have wellbeing and socio-economic benefits for individuals, but also presents a compelling financial case for schools and providers of education.

Working Flexibly During Menopause

Whilst many women leave their professional roles because of menopause, others turn to part-time working. Yet in teaching, requests to work part-time are not as likely to be accepted compared to the wider labour market (NASUWT, 2016). Bazeley et al. (2022) found that 14% of the women they surveyed, from a variety of professions, had reduced their working hours due to menopause. Working part-time, even if offered, can come with drawbacks – the most obvious is that there will be a reduction in pay, which might immediately rule it out as an option for many. Other downsides include impacts on pensions and loss of promotion possibilities. Mid-life is when women are most likely to be in, or aspiring to, positions of school leadership or other career progression routes (Booth et al., 2021).

Suzanne's research (Brown, 2019) shone a new light on how part-time working can be detrimental to chances of achieving senior leadership positions. Her own experience of requesting part-time working led to her request being granted, but with the proviso that she relinquished her Head of Faculty position. Sadly, we hear of similar stories regularly.

Other forms of flexible working exist (Patience and Rose, 2022), and are widely used outside of the school sector to support women through menopause, yet school leaders appear to find these difficult to accommodate (Sharp et al., 2019). This is concerning because offering flexible working is suggested as a way to improve teacher retention (See et al., 2020; Worth and Faulkner-Ellis, 2022).

Hybrid working (working some hours from home, some on-site) has been increasingly taken up since the Covid-19 pandemic. Katy's research with University Professional Services staff (Marsh-Davies, 2023) revealed that women in menopause found hybrid working tremendously beneficial. Enabling teachers to work from home when not timetabled to be in the classroom could be part of an arsenal of measures that education workplaces could adopt. This would fit with expectations of good work in the post-Covid era, but cultures of presenteeism stubbornly persist. Menopause leave has also been utilised by some corporate organisations and could be adopted within educational settings to enable a temporary pause to manage symptoms and re-energise.

All of these options *could* support teachers during menopause but, as well as the risks to these women financially and career-wise, they render women in mid-life less visible in schools, especially as senior leaders. It would be a shame to lose their experience, their talent and their ability to be role models for younger colleagues and pupils. We therefore argue that school leaders need to be more creative in the flexible working approaches they offer, as sometimes small, informal, and temporary changes can make a huge impact.

Having structures which encourage communication about changes in life circumstances, and conversations around different ways of working flexibly, can support all colleagues at different stages of their lives. This seems a vital part of an empathetic and caring working culture.

To conclude, making opportunities for supportive conversations, as well as creative solutions to enable working flexibly, seem an important way of enabling workplace cultures which are empathetic, not only to those trying to manage their menopause transition, but also to the wider workforce at points in their lives when support and understanding might be required.

Disruptions

- Enabling experienced, talented, and committed women to stay in the workforce is an important way of addressing teacher retention. If teachers remain in the profession this also helps to address the recruitment crisis by not needing to recruit as many teachers.
- Flexible working is not uncommitted working. Suzanne's research (Brown, 2019) revealed the valuable contributions those who work flexibly bring to teaching, and these need to be recognised and celebrated.
- Supporting access to different and appropriate ways of working flexibly seems crucial in attracting people to the profession and keeping them. The espoused values of schooling are around equality and fulfilling potential of pupils, so we have a moral obligation to do this for those who work in schools too. There is too much to lose if we don't.

To conclude, making opportunities for supportive conversations, as well as creative solutions to enable working flexibly, seem an important way of enabling workplace cultures that are empathetic, not only to those trying to manage their menopause transition, but also to the wider workforce at points in their lives when support and understanding might be required.

References

Bazeley, A., Marren, C. and Sheperd, A. (2022) *Menopause and the workplace* [Online]. Available at: www.fawcettsociety.org.uk/Handlers/Download.ashx?IDMF=9672cf45-5f13-4b69-8882-1e5e643ac8a6 (accessed 20 June 2023).

Booth, J., Coldwell, M., Müller, L. M., Perry, E. and Zuccollo, J. (2021) 'Mid-careers teachers: A mixed methods scoping study of professional development, career progression and retention', *Education Sciences*, 11(16), 299.

Brewis, J., Beck, V., Davies, A. and Matheson, J. (2017) 'Menopause transition: effects on women's economic participation', *University of Bristol* [Online]. Available at: https://

research-information.bris.ac.uk/en/publications/menopause-transition-effects-on-womens-economic-participation (accessed 30 April, 2024).

British Menopause Society (2021) *Response to the Department of Health and Social Care's call for evidence to help inform the development of the government's Women's Health Strategy* [Online]. Available at: https://thebms.org.uk/2021/08/the-british-menopause-society-response-to-the-department-of-health-and-social-cares-call-for-evidence-to-help-inform-the-development-of-the-governments-womens-health-strateg/ (accessed 22 June 2023).

Brown, S. (2019) Part-time Women Teachers and their Career Progression: A Life History Approach. Doctoral thesis, Sheffield Hallam University. Available at: https://doi.org/10.7190/shu-thesis-00256 (accessed 25 March 2024).

Education Support (2023) *Managing the menopause at school: Your stories* [Online]. Available at: www.educationsupport.org.uk/resources/for-individuals/articles/managing-the-menopause-at-school-your-stories/ (accessed 26 July 2023).

MacArthur, S. (2021) 'Menopause in education: The impact on the teaching profession', *Diverse Educators*, 23 March [Online]. Available at: www.diverseeducators.co.uk/menopause-in-education-the-impact-on-the-teaching-profession/ (accessed 26 July 2023).

Marsh-Davies, K. (2023) Unpublished report to client: Experiences of hybrid working during menopause.

NASUWT (2016) *Flexible working: The experience of teachers* [Online]. Available at: www.nasuwt.org.uk/static/uploaded/6fd07ce3-6400-4cb2-a8a87b736dc95b3b.pdf (accessed 15 September 2023).

Organisation for Economic Co-operation and Development (OECD) (2021) *Education at a glance 2021: OECD indicators* [Online]. Available at: www.oecd-ilibrary.org/sites/892d714e-en/index.html?itemId=/content/component/892d714e-en#chapter-d1e29682 (accessed 26 July 2023).

Patience, L. and Rose, L. (2022) *Flex Education*. London: Sage/Corwin.

See, B. H., Morris, R., Gorard, S., Kototsaki, D. and Abdi, S. (2020) 'Teacher recruitment and retention: A critical review of international evidence of most promising interventions', *Education Sciences*, 10(10), 262.

Sharp, C., Smith, R., Worth, J. and Van den Brande, J. (2019) *Part-time Working and Flexible Working in Secondary Schools*. Slough: NFER.

Steffan, B. (2021) 'Managing menopause at work: The contradictory nature of identity talk', *Gender, Work and Organization*, 28(1), 195–214.

Worth, J. (2023) *Short supply: Addressing the post-pandemic teacher supply challenge in England* [Online]. Available at: www.nfer.ac.uk/short-supply-addressing-the-post-pandemic-teacher-supply-challenge-in-england/ (accessed 26 July 2023).

Worth, J. and Faulkner-Ellis, H. (2022) *The teacher labour market in England: Annual report 2022* [Online]. Available at: www.nfer.ac.uk/teacher-labour-market-in-england-annual-report-2022/ (accessed 17 November 2022).

26

WHAT'S YOUR PROBLEM WITH FLEXIBLE WORKING?

Wendy Cobb and Dr Kerry Jordan-Daus

KEY POINTS

This chapter will:

- disrupt normalised working practices that fail to value flexible working and reconceptualise constructs of leadership
- provide powerful personal narratives to clarify the positive impact of flexible working
- empower leaders to make system-wide changes
- challenge established practice and make flexible working the new normal.

Introduction: The Times They Are A-Changing

This chapter addresses one of the most important educational issues of our time – flexible working. Let's be clear, flexible working is much more than 'part-time'; in England it encompasses, for example, 'staggered hours, compressed hours or working from home' (Department for Education, 2019: 7). It's the answer to our recruitment and retention crisis. It's an answer to the loss of women with caring responsibilities, to colleagues who want a phased retirement, to those who want to regain a work–life balance or finish that Master's in Education. There is an abundance of evidence to support the claim that flexible working is the future, yet the research evidence to advocate for its wider implementation in the education sector is sparse. Our case studies add to this evidence base.

In their most recent literature review, the Department for Education (2019: 19) argue the responsibility for the lack of flexible working opportunities lies with school leaders:

> The most common challenge to implementing flexible working practices in schools cited within research studies, and anecdotally, is a perceived lack of support for flexible working among school leadership teams.

Let us also be clear: we can all make a request for flexible working; it is our legal right. So, why isn't it more prevalent in the education sector? The aim of this chapter is to illustrate, through our case studies, the value of embracing flexibility as a usualised feature of organisations' recruitment and retention strategy. We want to disrupt thinking and practice that, in short, is contributing to the loss of too many of our valued colleagues, and at a time when reported vacancies are growing. We have a recruitment and retention crisis. But we also have a solution: flexible working is the future. This chapter will demonstrate how flexible working has retained, empowered and unleashed women leaders, who could otherwise have left our profession. These women are leaving the profession (Simons, 2016; Sheppard and Campbell, 2023), but it is within our collective gift to stop this.

> We've convinced the naysayers that flexible working really works – and that people, and in particular women, are not at home shirking, but are working productively while still having the connection with home and family. (Anne Fancke OBE, CEO, Chartered Management Institute UK, cited in Burnford, 2022)

The education sector is behind in the game when it comes to flexible working. Our message is it's time to catch up!

'I Should Be So Lucky!'

Wendy came into teaching as a second career (previously personnel management) after spending nine years at home raising two boys, during which time she studied languages and worked voluntarily in schools alongside other voluntary work and homeworking in the evenings. Looking back 15 years, Wendy 'felt lucky' that a succession of Headteachers encouraged her to take on creative curriculum leadership roles. However, she was soon exhausted after long hours in the classroom and more hours planning and marking at the weekend, with barely the energy or time to join the rest of the family for a trip to the park or to drag the vacuum cleaner over an increasingly messy house. When she first mentioned total exhaustion, after being commended for her clear passion for teaching and learning at a yearly appraisal, and a desire to go part-time, the Headteacher's immediate response was 'Get a cleaner!'. She was therefore surprised when she casually mentioned part-time working as a utopian dream at her next appraisal, that her new appraiser, her year leader, immediately stepped into the role of advocate and insisted that it must happen and that she would sort it, which she promptly did. After four years of full-time working, during which time she was unable to attend any daytime events at her children's schools, Wendy recalls the intense joy she felt during her first term of part-time working at securing a front-row seat at her youngest child's Christmas concert, where she sat watching him tentatively play 'Little Donkey' on the piano.

Wendy found that she had a renewed passion for teaching once she adopted a 0.8 contract. She describes missing her class and bouncing into school on Monday morning. She took up every opportunity for professional development and became a leading teacher. This led to a contract with the local authority to lead on primary languages development alongside another part-time teaching role. She subsequently took on a variety of leadership positions, including school governance, deputy head part-time, initial teacher education programme lead, leadership coach, local authority advisor and independent educational consultant. She also studied for a Master's in Leadership of management and learning.

It's worth reflecting on why it is that Wendy 'felt lucky' in her career. Is this because the culture of the education sector privileges presentism? Wendy's leadership was unleashed when other leaders recognised her initiatives and how she influenced others. Wendy was a change agent. She could have left the profession, but the system leaders offered different and intentional new constructs of leadership. The leaders created a new senior leadership position which embraced flexible working. Today, Wendy still experiences inflexibility even though her caring circumstances have significantly changed recently. Yet she feels empowered to use her voice to present a clear rationale for flexible working, as to how it benefits both her own circumstances and the organisation.

'Two is Better Than One!'

Deputy Headteachers Lisa and Lauren have been able to build both their careers and enjoy their caring roles with young children. As they talk about their Deputy Head leadership roles, they can see the personal and organisational benefits. The division of responsibilities certainly plays to their professional strengths. They might describe themselves as 'lucky', as their experiences of leadership are not widely replicated across our education sector. Their school has been adaptive and creative in constructing their contracts, giving both flexibility with how they manage their professional and personal lives. Their school, in an area of high social deprivation, has retained two outstanding women leaders. The Headteacher and governors have embraced flexible working.

Lauren has taken on additional responsibilities as her children have got older. This year, it felt right to embark on her National Professional Qualification Headship. She is now ready to lead her own school. She is acutely aware of how the flexible leadership structure has enabled her to take on a range of leadership projects, but always to fit into her 0.8 contract. Lauren's days are compressed to enable her to fulfil her multiple roles of parent, Deputy Head Teacher and the Special Education Needs Coordinator. Lauren's flexible contract enables her to do the school drop off and pick up and attend school events without guilt or having to request time off.

Lisa has a 0.6 Deputy Head Curriculum Lead role. With one child in pre-school and one in reception, Lisa has multiple roles. She has a very significant responsibility, planning the implementation of curriculum across the school, line-management of phase leads and accountability for pupils' outcomes. Lisa also teaches one day a week.

The job share with Lauren is a ying and yang collaboration. Lisa is not looking for Headship yet, but the flexibility of her contract has enabled her to continue in a significant leadership role. Equally, since flexible working is applied at the leadership level, it gives a strong organisational message that this is usual.

In discussion with Lauren, her career has been able to develop because others saw her leadership potential. She has gradually taken on additional leadership responsibilities, including further study. Lisa worked hard to build her career and didn't want to give it up because she became a mother. The flexible working opportunities afforded have given Lisa a choice.

The multiple roles we have place a strain on all of us, and the usual solution may be to reduce. However, multiple role enhancement theory recognises the uplift that multiple roles can have on an individual's wellbeing and sense of agency (Quach, 2017).

Another very important issue to flag is both have been able to continue to progress on the Leadership Pay Scale. Because they are working flexibly they are no less skilled, and their hourly level of remuneration should not be less because they work fewer hours. The education sector gender pay gap will continue to be one of the worst in the United Kingdom (Guibourg, 2018) until we challenge these outmoded assumptions that flexible working offers less value.

Disruptions

- System leaders, be 10% braver and confidently use your positions to be the change agents and communicate clearly why the future must include flexible working: we cannot continue to haemorrhage skilled practitioners and leaders.
- System leaders, make at least one change today: for example, include on every job advert that you offer flexible working.
- Flexible workers, tell your stories and join with us to communicate the positive personal and organisational benefits of flexible working.
- Everyone, challenge practices that discriminate against flexible working.

References

Burnford, J. (2022) *Don't Fix Women: The Practical Path to Gender Equality at Work*. Northwich: Practical Inspiration Publishing.

Department for Education (DfE) (2019) *Exploring flexible working practice in schools: Literature review* [Online]. Available at: www.gov.uk/government/publications (accessed 17 July 2023).

Guibourg, C. (2018) 'Gender pay gap: Six things we've learnt', *BBC News*, 7 April [Online]. Available at: www.bbc.co.uk/news/business-43668187 (accessed 17 July 2023).

Quach, E. D. (2017) Multiple Roles in Later Life: Role Enhancement and Conflict and their Effects on Psychological Wellbeing. PhD thesis, University of Massachusetts Boston. Available at: https://core.ac.uk/download/pdf/229368115.pdf (accessed 24 July 2023).

Sheppard, E. and Campbell, G. (2023) 'We're on the road to nowhere: Women aged 30–39 – why are they the largest demographic to leave teaching every year?', *Impact*, 31 January [Online]. Available at: https://my.chartered.college/impact_article/were-on-a-road-to-nowhere-women-aged-30-39-why-are-they-the-largest-demographic-to-leave-teaching-every-year/ (accessed 24 July 2023).

Simons, J. (ed.) (2016) *The Importance of Teachers: A Collection of Essays on Teacher Recruitment and Retention*. London: Policy Exchange [Online]. Available at: https://policyexchange.org.uk/publications/ (accessed 23 July 2023).

CASE STUDY 6

NEGOTIATING FLEXIBLE WORKING

UPHOLDING YOUR PRINCIPLES

Maggie Eldridge-Mrotzek

As an education adviser, pre-Covid, I had considerable flexibility with my place of work and times of my working hours to attend to projects, visit schools, research, and write reports. It was quite a shock post-Covid, when many staff had been working in a more hybrid model, that my line manager required a return to the office.

Post-Covid I had reassessed my caring responsibilities and my work–life relationship and realised that office working, presenteeism and the lack of valuing difference was not the model I wished to follow. I desired to continue to work flexibly while adhering to business and organisational requirements.

I was aware my organisation had a flexible working policy and decided to investigate. Eureka, I thought when I discovered the many different types of flexible working. I applied to my line manager initially, face to face, followed up with a formal written request for compressed hours, with every tenth day being my compressed day with some flexibility in the exact working hours of the other days. My direct manager refused my request. The reasons for refusal were not those stated in the policy but included views such as lack of availability in an emergency and increasing workload for others. My line manager had unfortunately not understood that flexible working would mean that neither of these concerns would be a barrier. I often accepted requests and phone calls at many different times of the day and I would continue to attend diligently and effectively to my work.

Action

I examined closely my organisation's policy, and as suggested in the policy, I appealed against the initial decision to a more senior manager. Polite replies were received referring to a lack of time to consider and consult with those directly involved with my work. After four months, and my case being passed to another senior line manager, my appeal was refused again.

I reached out to my local tribunal service for employee relations. The tribunal confirmed that guidelines as in my organisation's flexible working policy had not been followed: no meeting had been undertaken with myself, statutory timelines had not been adhered to and the reasons for refusal were not those that applied in law. I also reached out to my network, should I need testimonials about my work. I approached two outstanding Headteachers who, without hesitation, agreed to support me if required. This time was personally stressful. I felt compelled now to set an example for others and to bring people who had ignored policy to account, and so to be 10% braver.

Result

Following negotiations, a new request for flexible working was made and agreed.

The organisation has honestly reviewed its flexible working policy and set out improved guidance for managers, including stronger timelines, discrete expectations and compulsory training workshops. The number of people being courageous to now apply for and be given flexible working in my organisation has increased. This has undoubtedly been a very positive wakeup call. It has led to increased benefits for the employer as well as the morale, work–life relationship and retention of valued staff.

Disruptions

- Know how to negotiate: in this case the different types of flexible working, and select one that suits you.
- Don't give reasons for your request unless you wish to. It is your entitlement to request flexible working in most working establishments.
- Ensure that the policy timelines are kept to.
- Check that any refusal to give flexible working or delay in responding is in line with the flexible working policy of your organisation.
- Don't be afraid to seek legal advice from the local tribunal service, citizens advice or your union to help you navigate the legal process and challenge if deemed appropriate.
- Network regularly with trusted colleagues who value you and can support or even vouch for you if required.
- Keep up with your life – exercise, good meals out, faith meetings, connecting with friends and other activities that give you joy.
- Remember you are magnificent in whatever your role in education: leading, supporting, teaching, and empowering pupils and colleagues. Following years of study, gathering experience, supporting and leading others, you deserve to be valued!

For line managers/senior leaders

- When a request from your colleagues arrives on your desk, in this case for flexible work, make an appointment to talk to the person to understand what would work best for them.
- Plan an approach together that meets organisational and operational needs.
- Develop a whole organisational team-based approach.
- Develop or amend corporate policy and check it mirrors the stated values of your organisation.

CASE STUDY 7

THE BIG WHEEL OF FLEXIBLE WORKING

Aimee Quickfall

Aimee Quickfall shares Sabah's story.

Sabah tells me a story about part-time working. She laughs through most of it. To give some context, Sabah had been working as a Key Stage 2 teacher in a large suburban primary school for ten years when she had her first child, Ben. Sabah returned to full-time work when Ben was six months old and realised that she was not comfortable spending 50 hours away from him a week, due to her hours at work and the commute.

My route to part-time work is like a big wheel ride, scary on the way up! I didn't know who to speak to really ... my experience was that part-time teachers were sort of frowned upon. I had a sense that it wasn't a welcome situation with the senior leadership team. I sounded out the deputy head, who I was quite close to, and she asked me if I could really afford to take the drop in salary. It was a fair question I suppose, I am a single mum. I was so worried that going part-time meant I was 'letting the side down' and that the rest of the staff would be disappointed with me.

I got myself in such a state about requesting part-time hours, that eventually even the Head noticed there was something wrong and called me in for a chat. He already knew what I was thinking about doing and said I needed to think carefully about it, as it would not be easy to find a job-share partner, I might not get on well with them if they could find someone, and that our parents would not find it easy to adjust to part-time staff.

I was gutted to be honest with you ... I didn't feel like I could continue working full-time when the day care was costing so much, and the time apart was messing up breastfeeding. On top of that, I was so tired all the time. I wanted to get off the ride.

In the end, I started looking out for other posts in schools closer to home. I went to look around a few and it just didn't click. Then I found Oakleaf School. The post was advertised as full-time but flexible working were terms available. I went to have a look around and the team were just so welcoming: there were already job-share partnerships working well in the school and the deputy head who showed me around said that the school really benefitted from having more views and ideas to draw upon, and a refreshed teacher coming in part way through the week.

Needless to say, I didn't get the job (!!) but another post came up at that school and I applied and got it.

I have been there for five years now and Ben is thriving and I am thinking about applying for a team leadership role. I feel like I should have fought my corner in my old school, but do you know what? It was probably time for a change, and even though it was scary with a new baby, I am really glad I went for it.

Names in this case study have been changed.

CASE STUDY 8

INCLUDING WOMEN

Maz Foucher

In my experience, many talented and experienced women are excluded from leadership roles simply due to the way that we are expected to work within education. Once they have children, assumptions are often made that everyone has the money to pay for full-time childcare or family available to provide this. For several reasons, I did not have either of these. I also didn't want to rely on other people to care for my children; I wanted a career, but I also wanted to be present both physically and emotionally for my children. For me to pursue my career in school leadership, I took on a flexible leadership role in my children's school.

For me, the next four years were the most fulfilling of my teaching career. Our Headteacher was a big advocate of flexible working: most of our leadership team were mums, most of whom worked part-time and also had children at the school. We all understood the challenges of being a working parent, so the flexible and supportive approach we created ensured we could all juggle the demands of our roles alongside the demands of our families.

In 2019, the Department for Education's findings stated that 74% of senior leaders 'who had implemented flexible working in their school felt that these arrangements had helped staff to manage their workload/work-life balance' and that 89% of teachers who had experienced flexible working agreed with this (Department for Education, 2019: 11).

This certainly fits with my experience of working this way. Our working hours and roles were reviewed regularly to ensure our hours met our family and financial needs and our job-share partners supported us in our teaching roles. We were creative with our timetables to ensure we were all working to our subject strengths and ensured that our days overlapped at least once a week so that we could meet regularly. There was always someone ready to step in without judgement whenever one of our children was ill or a family emergency occurred. There's an old saying that it takes a village to raise a child; our school become our village and I am immensely grateful to all the incredible women I worked with during this time.

What is more, we were successful in our outcomes: results across the school improved and we secured the school's first good Ofsted judgement in over ten years. Personally, I believe this success stemmed from the huge emotional investment we all had in the work we were doing and the fact that none of us had the parental guilt of missing out on our children's childhood while doing so. Now that my children have moved on to secondary school, I can look back and evaluate the pros and cons of this experience. Overall, I believe it was positive for us as a family; I believe we are closer for having had these years together. It enabled me to celebrate with them when school was going well and intervene swiftly when they were finding things tricky. Socially, it was difficult for us at times, but sticking to a few key friendships with families we could trust made things a lot easier. Both of my children have a great understanding of the education system, as well as empathy for their teachers. I believe this has enabled them to tread the secondary school path more carefully. It hasn't been without its issues, but overall, it worked out well for us all.

Reference

Department for Education (2019) *Exploring flexible working practice in schools Interim report*. Available at: https://assets.publishing.service.gov.uk/government/uploads/system/uploads/attachment_data/file/938784/Exploring_flexible_working_practice_in_schools_-_interim_report.pdf (accessed 26 March 2024).

INDEX